HANDMADE TOYS AND GAMES

A GUIDE TO CREATING YOUR OWN

Other books by Jean Ray Laury

Frontis, Ferry Boat, 20", by Rob Denny.

HANDMADE
TOYS AND GAMES

A GUIDE TO CREATING YOUR OWN

by Jean Ray Laury

and Ruth Milliken Law

Doubleday & Company, Inc., Garden City, New York, 1975

We wish to acknowledge our indebtedness to all the children
who have encouraged us by their response to our work,
and to all craftsmen, who are quite serious about play.

Editorial Director: Rachel Martens, Crafts Editor, *Farm Journal*, Inc.
All works by the authors unless otherwise credited.
Drawings: Jean Ray Laury
Photographs: Gayle Smalley unless otherwise credited.

Library of Congress Cataloging in Publication Data

Laury, Jean Ray
    Handmade toys and games

        1. Toy making. 2. Games.   I. Law, Ruth Milliken, joint author.
II. Title.
TT174.L38   745.59'2
ISBN 0-385-07180-9
Library of Congress Catalog Card Number 73–81124

Contents

HANDMADE TOYS AND GAMES

A GUIDE TO CREATING YOUR OWN

1 *Rolls-Royce, 18" long, by Doug Parmeter.*

Introduction

TOYS ARE FOR EVERYONE

Who can walk past a toyshop without casting a longing gaze inside? Toys must possess some magic charm by which they evoke memories and nostalgic recollections from us all. Anyone who at age three, thirty, or eighty-three has an inquisitive mind, a receptive nature, or an adventurous spirit, will find pleasure in toys. Who can resist this invitation to play?

Play is an essential activity for all human beings. After watching bear cubs, kittens, or tree squirrels, you know that play is not limited to people. But toys are—and toys offer many kinds of play and many ways of playing.

A good toy expands potentials, or extends horizons. It creates an atmosphere for fantasy. The toy need not be elaborate or expensive or complex. Watch a toddler explore a box of tissues or a loaf of bread and you know the kind of delight to be found in these everyday household objects.

What people consider appropriate and what they provide for their children to play with tells much about their values. At present the plethora of self-absorbed, electronic, battery-operated, internally complex toys surely reflects the involvement of many people with the technology of the age. These toys do not necessarily relate to children's needs regarding toys. Whether the adults of a society are mainly engaged in farming or in working long hours in a factory, their children's needs are similar. Children look for challenge and for the opportunity to discover, to explore, to find out things on their own. As a by-product of this explorative play they develop muscles through the manipulation of objects, learn comparison and contrast, develop number and color concepts, and learn size and shape relationships. Most commercial toys contribute little to these needs. "Playing" becomes synonymous with switch turning and battery changing. If a five-year-old "needs" a mechanical teen-age dancing doll with blue eye shadow, it is surely an externally imposed need. Helping or allowing a small child to make his own fantasy props is more to the point. Given the materials with help only as needed, children themselves are imaginative, prolific, and successful toymakers.

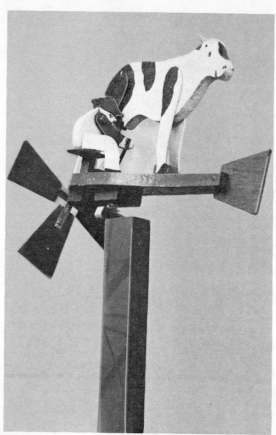

2 *Wind Toy, 14″, designer unknown.*

3 *Crane, 20″ cab, by Rob Denny.*

4 *Bag Swing by Jean Ray Laury.*

Making toys also fulfills certain adult needs. Perhaps with our inability to recapture our childhoods, to be children again, making toys is the next best thing. Certainly a toymaker needs to have some personal feeling of what it is like to play with the toy he makes.

Most toys distill some essence from objects in the adult world. The toymaker must recognize that essence and retain it while discarding all that is extraneous. He can take liberties with size, scale, pattern, sound, materials, weight, and texture, but the essential character must remain. Exactly what the essential character is, the toymaker knows when he has found it . . . as does the person who picks up the toy. It is not the same thing for every toymaker—or for every child (or adult) who plays with it.

One distinction between the well-loved toy and the discarded toy is the extent to which the toy assumes a recognizable form. A child may pick up a scrap of wood that happens to be the right proportion, and you hear his "rhummm, rhummm" as he starts up the motor to drive it off. Absence of wheels is no deterrent. Imaginative and creative play surround the simplest forms. The essence of a car, for a child, may be the steering wheel and horn, or four places to sit, or the noise of the engine.

There is room in the world for all kinds of toys. The block of wood will suffice as an auto, but the same child may cherish a more ornately carved and painted one. We can all enjoy both baked potatoes and vichyssoise without abandoning one for the other.

A good toy, then, is a beginning, not an end. It suggests and invites activity, handling, or play. It makes play possible by extending an invitation to exercise bodily, to manipulate the toy, or to enjoy mental gymnastics. It stirs a muscle or the brain to activity. The potential of a toy, then, is what makes it exciting . . . it has possibilities. If it is also tactually satisfying or visually exquisite or mechanically ingenious, we are doubly fortunate. The whistle, while it may be a beautiful sculptured form, comes to full flower when someone blows on it. A swing, however elegantly made, comes alive when someone jumps on it and rides. Even the teddy bear must acknowledge some sense of fulfillment when it's hauled off to nap time. Why else are all of us more sentimental about a patched and battered teddy bear than the new one on the toy shelf?

EVERYONE CAN BE A TOYMAKER

What we have offered here is an elaborate and surely irresistible invitation to everyone to become a toymaker . . . to make a toy. You begin, as we did, with the assumption that toys are worthwhile—not just for children, who might be the recipients of your toys, but for you. Adults show themselves to be just older and larger children in many ways. What this has come to mean to us is that pull toys for adults must have longer strings than those for children.

This book is for toymakers of all ages, and for all degrees of skill and

5 *Welded Steel Car, 5",*
by Rick Columbini.

6 *Propeller Car, 4",*
by Tom Freund.

7 Wood Castle, 21″, by Michael Hughes.

experience. The most talented wood carver or the most competent stitcher will enjoy the first efforts of the five-year-old toymaker . . . and vice versa!

Much of the joy in toymaking is within the process itself. The finished product may bring delight or pleasure or amusement, but so must the work itself. We propose to give you a mental or visceral tickle —to stimulate your own interest in toymaking.

This book is not meant to be a comprehensive survey of toys or toymaking. It offers, rather, a refreshing look at some of the toys people are making today in this country. A great many people, young and old, are obviously having a perfectly wonderful time. They have generously and joyfully shared their efforts and their thoughts with you.

Merely settling on some kind of organization necessary to get this all on paper was rather perplexing. As soon as we separated wheeled things from stuffed things in a logical way, Lenore Schwartz Goodell sent us a stuffed fabric train. After we separated blocks from figures, Arthur Lind sent stacking blocks in the shape of people. We had all these categories, and then some of the most imaginative people on earth sent us toys that didn't fit any group at all, and wouldn't, regardless of our efforts at grouping. Well, good for them and good for everybody.

The toys in this book are made by experienced, trained people with expert know-how—and by inexperienced, untrained amateurs. Some are the work of people who talk for hours about what they do and why, and others by those whose communication is so completely in their work that they feel no need to verbalize. Some of the toys are for adults, some are for children. They are the work of young and old —of people with a keen interest in technical excellence, and of people with a keen idea of what their toy was to be, coupled with a fine indifference to technique. The toys produced by such a wide range of interests stand on their own merits. Each has its own value. Perhaps this wide range of approaches is related to the even wider range of uses to which children put their toys.

Begin where you are. Sharpen your eye to what is around you. Make a toy for yourself (there's somebody you can count on). Start with familiar materials. If you have experience in sewing or in woodworking, you know something about the nature of the materials used and the techniques available. Or forget that and play with something you have never handled before—clay or metal. Vacuum cleaners, sanders, sewing machines, drills, electric mixers, and saws are all just tools. If you have used any of them, you can use all of them.

We have collected here a dazzling array of what some people did with their humor, wit, creative urges, and scraps of this and that. At any rate, anyone with a playful gene should feel encouraged (even inspired!) by these toys to have a try at making his own.

8 Rattle, 7", by Gordon Brofft.

9 Bear-in-race-car Whistle, 3",
by Bill Horgos.

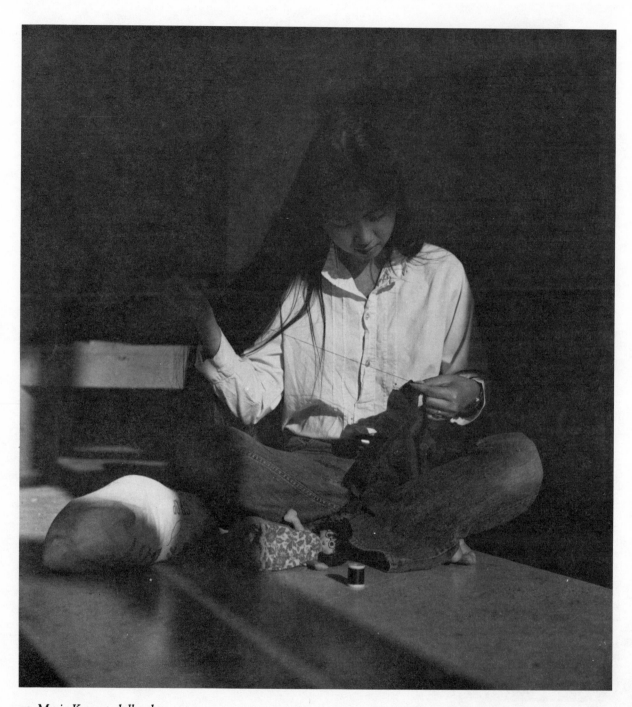

10 *Maria Kwong, dollmaker.*

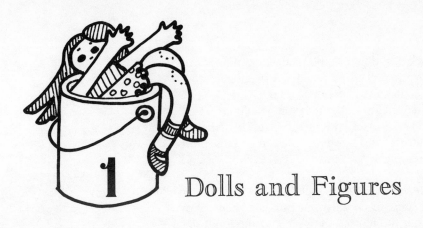

Dolls and Figures

Surely there is no more beloved toy than the doll—and probably no toy is more fun to make. History is full of stories of children's devotion to dolls. This is understandable since a doll is a people-replica and is often thought of as a "real" person by its owner.

Dolls *do* take on personalities as they are constructed. They serve as tolerant and accepting friends, traveling companions, punch bags, scapegoats, whipping boys, confidantes, and pillows. They seem to be equally lovable in the form of flawless infants, sleek glamour girls (or boys), kids like oneself, Pillsbury Dough, Raggedy Ann, Green Giants, or the Raisin Bran Doll. Many doll lovers never lose their interest in dolls, although the *nature* of that interest may change. Doll clubs are centers of feverish activity by lovers and collectors of varied interests relating to dolls.

Dolls can be made of practically anything. There are very few people in the world who can't manage a scrap of wadded cloth, tied off near one end to make a head and body. Mark a face on the head and you have the simplest doll imaginable, infinitely better than none at all. The dolls we've photographed to show in this book are made of a wide variety of materials—fabric, wood and leather, crochet yarn, nylons, felt, spools, clothespins, and apples. Some have been made by children with sure instincts about what their dolls should look like. Some are first dolls, some are the work of experienced craftsmen. Some are one of a kind, while others were turned out in batches. Wood clothespin dolls, for instance, tend to run in gangs—nobody makes just one clothespin doll.

A wide range of materials is available for dollmaking—from easy-to-use felt to woven stretch-knit or bonded fabrics, both washable and non-washable. Hair can be added by latching, hooking, braiding, knitting, or crocheting with yarns; or by using strips of fabric, fur, wire, and perhaps even some of your own hair. Buttons, felt shapes, and embroidery stitches can make a face.

Dolls can be made from one piece of fabric, such as a sock, or from two pieces, a front and a back. Or they can be made in a number of pieces with head, arms, and legs attached to a body. Also, there are all kinds of insets and tailoring details to consider or to ignore.

All the foregoing refers only to cloth dolls. It is impossible to list all the other materials available for the eager, enterprising, and imaginative dollmaker. For your first doll, try what appeals most or seems most possible. If you make one doll, you are sure to make another and another and another.

The easiest doll to make may start with a sock, as shown in Plates 11 and 12. There are several ways to do this, but ours are made with the head and body formed from the foot of the sock and the legs from the sock top. See Drawing 1. The doll's arms and hat can be made from the other sock of the pair. Use cotton or polyester batting to stuff the doll; embroidery stitches to define a face.

The easiest fabric to use is felt because it does not ravel. It is easy to sew by hand or by machine, and it can be finished with a seam on the outside, carefully trimmed after the seam is made. See Drawing 2. A felt doll is suggested in Color Plate 17.

Woven fabrics must have the seam on the wrong side to conceal raw edges, as in Drawing 3. Leave an opening for stuffing. Turn the doll right side out after sewing it, stuff it, and close the opening by hand. Plates 13 and 14 show a simple doll cut in two pieces, with the seam on the wrong side.

Close scrutiny of Maria's dolls in Plates 15 through 18 shows that Maria has mastered the problem of sewing a narrow body part by clipping the seam allowance and turning the part right side out for stuffing. The smaller and more detailed the parts, the more difficult to sew. Thus, a mitten-type hand is easier to make than a glove-type hand. Dolls made with one piece for the front and one for the back, then stuffed, tend to be stiff, as in Plate 19. Making arms and legs separate and attaching them provides for more flexibility, as in Plates 20–23 and Drawing 4.

A third alternative is shown in Plate 24, where an elaborately dressed doll reveals a seam across her knee. This has the same effect as making her leg in two pieces so that it can bend at the knee. See Drawing 5. A button sewn between leg and body, as illustrated in Drawing 6, provides for greater flexibility.

The figure in Plate 27 shows how little this kind of detail might matter. She is made of undoll-like herringbone weave fabric—"a little scratchy as moms sometimes are." Legs and body are cut in one piece, and wormlike arms are attached. What matters most with this doll is her thoughtful admonition to "Take good care of your body, you can use it over and over again." It was made as a kind of life-preserver by a mother of six "to remind the kids that if they didn't push too hard, they'd get more mileage out of Mom."

The red-haired hayseed in Plate 33 (he fears he is coming down with something) is made from a nylon stocking and batting. For the small head shown, use the toe or foot of the hosiery. For a larger head, the open end of the stocking is tied off and stuffed. The head and body are usually made in one piece (as with the sock doll), the stocking stuffed first to form a tube, then tied at the neck. Arms and legs can

11, 12 *Cloth dolls made from a pair of socks. Toe of sock becomes doll's head; arms and legs are made from cuff of sock. 20",
by Jude Martin.*

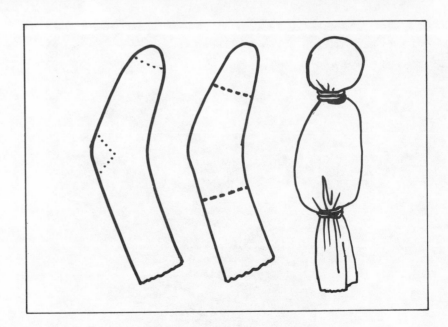

Drawing 1 *Socks may be readily and easily converted to doll shapes with stuffing by tying off areas to delineate head and body sections.*

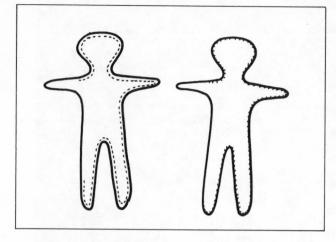

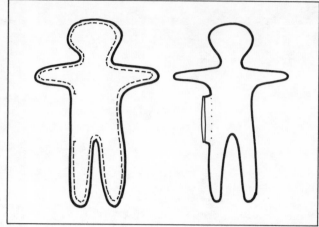

Drawing 2 Two identical body parts cut from felt are the beginnings of a simple doll form. Because felt does not ravel, the seams can be sewn on the outside. Machine stitch or whip stitch by hand.

Drawing 3 Use of woven fabric requires sewing on wrong side and turning seam. Leave space to insert stuffing and close by hand stitching.

13, 14 Dolls are sewn on wrong side of fabric; turned right side out. Stitched features peer out from under heavy yarn hair. Knotted cord suggests clasped hands. 5" to 9", by Jude Martin.

15 The astonishing hair on Maria Kwong's first doll is of small copper springs.

16 Brown fabric doll made in two-piece construction was sewn and turned, then stuffed. Hair is yarn, and facial features are stitched. 19", by Maria Kwong.

17 Sister Doll, in shocking pink, has hair of black yarn. Face and glasses are embroidered. She lies in a box lid made up to be her bed. 8", by Maria Kwong.

18 Batch of Kwong dolls all have two-piece bodies with yarn hair.

19 Acrylic paint on fabric adds colorful face and hair on 5″ doll, from Northwest Crafts Fair, Seattle, Washington.

20 (Below) Rag doll, with red and white yarn hair and button eyes. By Ruth Law.

21 Rag doll body made from multistriped knitted sweater. By Ruth Law.

22 First seven of "100 dolls" made from children's old stretch-knit clothing, saved for the purpose. 16″ to 20″, by Ruth Law.

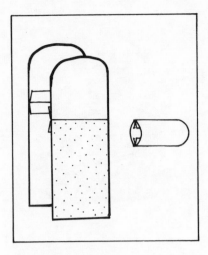

Drawing 4 *Simple form of arch shape for head and body. Small arches are used for arms and legs.*

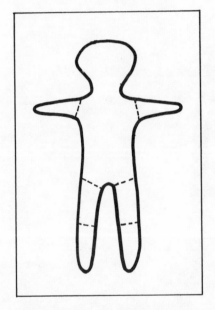

Drawing 5 *Stuff outer portion of arms and legs, then make a seam across before stuffing next section. Seams give arms and legs flexibility.*

23 *The body of this blue denim doll is the watch pocket from bib overalls. Hair is red felt cut in narrow strips and stitched on piece at a time. By Ruth Law.*

25 (Right) Moth Lady, a winged figure in cotton batik. 6″, by Elizabeth Fuller.

26 (Below) Elaborately embroidered doll is so completely covered with yarn and stitching that only the face reveals the basic fabric. Hair is embroidery floss, and features are suggested with a minimum of stitches. 8″, by Ingrid Petersen.

24 Jointed fabric doll has a merry face appliquéd directly to dress fabric. Her long thin arms and legs are stuffed and attached. Seams across leg at knee make this lady capable of many poses. 24″, by Gloria McNutt.

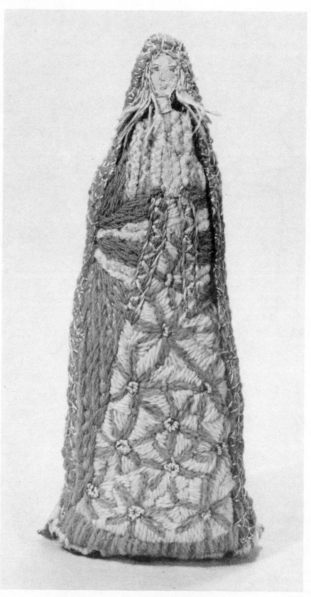

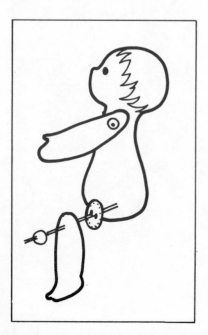

Drawing 6 Button fastened between body and leg allows for easy movement.

be made separately as in the "Hayseed," then stitched to the body. The dolls are pushy-soft and pliable, and much too lifelike for some people's tastes.

The lovable hag in Plate 32 has a cheeky head of nylon, complete with warts. Her black witch's garb reveals her calling, but it's obvious from her benign smile that she prefers casting love spells to curse putting. The teacher and child dolls in Plate 35 are made by forming the heads only of stuffed nylon. Lightweight cardboard rolled into a cone forms the body, then the head is stitched or taped to the top of the cone. Padding over the cardboard cone shapes the bodies. Face details are stitched, and unspun wool is added for the hair. Features as shown in Plate 34 are formed by stitching through the nylon, into the stuffing, and out again. As the thread is drawn tight, the features emerge in three dimensions.

Susan Morrison's Quaker Puffed Liberty in Color Plate 12 takes full advantage of the voluptuous possibilities of stuffed nylon. Lady Godiva is a stuffed cotton stocking, treated and stitched in the same way. See her perched side-saddle on her bay mount in Color Plate 6, ready for her famous horseback ride. Color Plate 13 shows another example using stitched nylon stockings.

Apple-head dolls take time and patience. The head in Color Plate 24 was made by carving a face on a freshly peeled apple, then letting it dry. Select a firm, hard apple for your doll head; avoid overripe, wormy or mealy fruit. Crisp, fresh Rome Beauties or Pippins are excellent. You must wait patiently for the face to age and emerge in its cured

27 ". . . and over again."
Whimsical doll with weak arms and a strong message is made of tweedy fabric. Casual hair is yarn; averted eyes of felt. 30",
by Margot Carter Blair.

28 Small stuffed doll has arms and legs jointed by stitching. Face details are appliquéd felt, and hair is braided yarn. 10",
by Bets Barnard.

29 Wide-eyed and convincingly virile, this weight lifter has so many bulges he can't fail. Strong Man, 32", by Susan Morrison.

30 Embroidered nose encircles button eyes. Incredible ears of really sympathetic listener are not stuffed. 17½", by Lenore Schwartz Goodell.

31 Kirstin's Doll is stuffed, loved, and washable. By Joyce Bossom Parmeter.

32 Benign witch, with warts, of stuffed nylon stocking. 12", by Jean Ray Laury.

33 *Features of stuffed nylon doll are brought into relief with pulled stitches, embroidery, and appliqué. Hair is red yarn. Note detailed nylon stuffed hands and felt shoes. 14", by Jean Ray Laury.*

state. For obvious reasons, apple dolls tend to look more like aged folk than like smooth youth. The apple-head peddler dolls shown in Plates 36 and 37 are the work of Alice Peterson. Alice builds her dolls on a corn husk base. One gets the feeling that she can cut any expression she chooses into an apple rather than wait to see what shows up in the drying. These ladies are decked out in glorious clothing far beyond their means. Plate 38 shows Annette Sutton's clothes-conscious witch carrying her traveling broom. The head is attached to a cardboard cone and her black clothing is sewn on permanently (witches do not change their clothes). She wears a regulation peaked witch hat, has wispy batting hair (as befits one of her years), and carries magic guinea feathers.

Many of us see little wooden people when we look at wood clothespins. Clotheslines are disappearing, and so are these wood clothespins. Even now they are as likely to be found in craft supply shops as in housewares departments. Some have even made their way into antique shops. Our group of clothespin dolls is the work of a half-dozen people. Clothespins can be sanded, undercoated, and painted like any other wood. Plate 39 and Color Plate 9 show people made in this way and painted with enamel. Plates 40 and 41, also enamel painted, show arms added as well as shoes or bases to make them stand. The girls in Plate 43 are all dressed with the aid of white household glue to hold fabric and embroidery thread in place. Faces and boots are drawn with a felt pen. The group in Plate 44 is more skillfully done, with elaborate hair styling and clothing. One lady has arms

34 *Toy Book Authors—details of two nylon/batting heads. By Jean Ray Laury.*

constructed into her clothing. Only the top half of the clothespin is needed for the baby.

Another traditional toy, illustrated in Drawing 7, takes only about fifteen seconds to make. A wound-up rubber band sets off a frantic wrestling match, which always ends in an exhausted stand-off.

Spools, like clothespins, provide a ready-made doll form. Plate 45 and Drawing 8 suggest some possible detailing.

With any kind of a fine-blade saw, wood dolls can be cut from flat pieces of wood. Provide a child with a pencil or felt pens and a chunk of half-inch clear pine, and he'll turn them out faster than you can saw. Plates 46 and 47 show doll designs drawn directly onto wood by small children.

Most boys and a surprising number of girls want to do their own sawing. The figures in Plates 50 and 51 are done by an eight-year-old boy who worked without help. No adult would have suggested the complexity of sawing out a flat shape, then standing the figure upright and sawing further details at right angles to the sawing just done. But that is the way the boy worked in shaping the water skier and fisherman.

35 (Opposite) Strait-laced teacher and reluctant student have stuffed nylon-stocking heads. Somber grays and browns of clothing reinforce general air of teacher's serious intent. School marm is 15½″ high, by Janet Spoecker.

36, 37 (Above) Ancient flower peddler is an apple-head doll elaborately decked out in lace and satin. Apple-head peddler carries a tiny basket of bread and a stick of pretzels. Each 14″, by Alice H. Peterson.

The old woman and her children who live in a felt shoe, Plate 53, are cut from clear pine, $5/16''$ thick, and painted in bright enamel colors. Such small figures as these, with so many colors and details, usually have to be completed in several steps. See them in full glorious color in Color Plate 20.

One of the most pleasing dolls ever is the simple, smooth little figure in Plate 54, made by Kay Gurule, of hardwood and leather thong. These were made as teaching aids for children to play with and talk about in preschools.

The chunky doll in Plates 55 and 56 was whittled by Maria Kwong. She calls it the Momo doll. *Momo* means "peach" in Japanese, and the doll is copied from a photo of Maria's mother as a child. The arms

38 *Grand old witch is an apple-face crone with wispy Dacron hair. She has an authentic corn husk and twig broom, guinea hen feathers. 12", by Annette Sutton.*

30

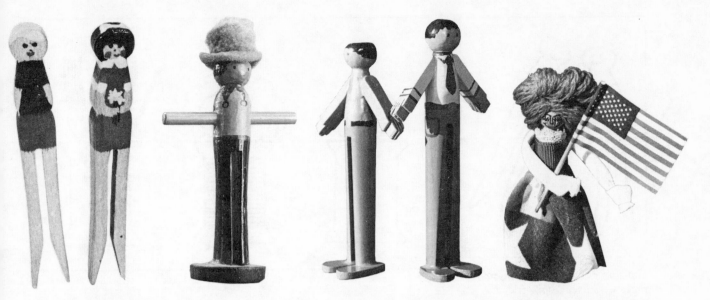

39 Miniature wood people, painted with acrylics, take advantage of contours of clothespins for figures. 2½", by Maria Kwong.

40, 41 (Above) Clothespin man has arms added—a dowel set into a hole drilled through the pin. He stands glued to a wood checker; his hat is one ball of fringe and a circle of felt. Two figures at right have arms and feet cut from thin pieces of pine. By Ruth Law.

42 Star print fabric and new flag held by knotted bias tape arms qualify this smiling lady to lead July 4th parade. By Jean Ray Laury.

43 Mod girls, dressed in fabric and embroidery thread, have features made with a felt pen. Clothes sewed and glued by eight-year-old Hilary Law.

44 Elegant ladies and small child are dressed in scraps of edgings and fabrics. Hair is yarn and batting. Wendy Northup simply cut off pin legs to make the baby.

Drawing 7 Two wood clothespins make wrestlers, despite friendly expressions. Twist pins in opposite directions and release for split-second grudge match as rubber band unwinds.

Drawing 8 Wood spools with nylon and batting-stuffed heads readily take on people shapes.

45 (Below) Small simple figures made of dowels, spools, and beads. 2½", by Ruth Law.

46 Child's drawing on wood, using permanent-color felt pens. Cut on jigsaw by adult. 4" high, by Alison Law at age six.

47 Marking pen drawing on wood. By Alison Law at age six.

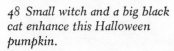

49 Artist's family as acrobats. Figures of mother, father, and two boys are all cut of same shape, with differentiating details painted on. Heads, hands, and feet are cut straight and level to make balancing possible. 3½" tall, by Jim Aiken.

48 Small witch and a big black cat enhance this Halloween pumpkin.

50 Balsa fisherman was drawn directly on wood and cut on jigsaw. Figure was then laid flat on its back so that head and neck could be trimmed at each side. By Joel Aiken at age eight.

51 Balsa water skier by an eight-year-old. After block figure was cut, it was stood on edge and hands were sawed out. Skis and tow bar are cut separately. Figure is water-colored. By Joel Aiken.

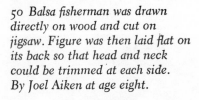

52 (Far right) A child's version of mother and baby.

53 *There was an old woman who lived in a fancy felt shoe (with Masonite inner sole!). She had so many enamel-painted wood children . . . 7" at roof line, by Ruth Law.*

54 *Softly contoured hardwood figure is an invitation to touch. Arms and legs are attached with knotted leather thongs. Dots burned into wood suggest face. 7½", by Kay Gurule.*

55, 56 *Momo doll is carved from clear pine and lacquered after sanding and painting. Hair and face are painted on. At right she is shown dressed. 7" tall, by Maria Kwong.*

and legs are attached with small screw eyes. Her hair, face, shoes, and socks are painted on.

Sherman Smith does not regard his dolls in Plates 57 and 58 as toys. Children find these figures attractive, although he makes them primarily for use by doll club members. They are whittled with movable mortise-and-tenon joints set with a tiny toothpick peg at the shoulders, elbows, hips, and knees. His Pinocchio may be one inch high or six inches high, but each is complete with movable joints. These dolls are a highly refined, contemporary version of the old "penny wooden" dolls whittled by New England sailors while at sea during American colonial days and made to be sold when the ships returned to port.

Arthur Lind's interest in toys led to a study of their history and social importance. When he turns off the lathe to talk, it is worthwhile listening. He has a very thoughtful approach to toymaking. Adults in other cultures place value on objects made for amusement,

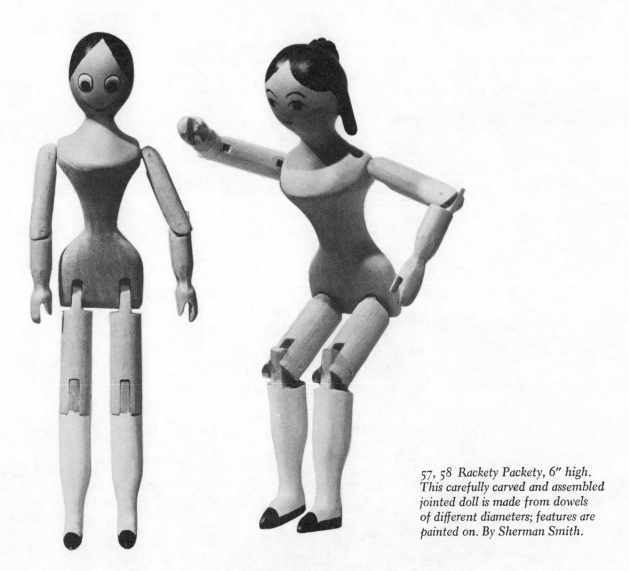

57, 58 Rackety Packety, 6" high. This carefully carved and assembled jointed doll is made from dowels of different diameters; features are painted on. By Sherman Smith.

and he thinks we should do this too. We deprive ourselves of something important when we relegate play to children only. The turned figures in Plate 64 are his work. He thinks we should all make our own toys because "the pleasure you get from making your own toys can't be bought from me."

The works of Doug Hansen and Sally Wetherby demonstrate just how much toys can mean to adults. Their creations are not without appeal for children, but one feels that adults would appreciate them more. Also, the toys are somewhat too fragile to be turned over to children; being able to do whatever you want with a toy (within reasonable limits) is important to children. Doug's Tower of Thrills, shown in Plates 59, 60 and 61 is an elaborate assemblage of wires, mirrors, hooks, doll parts, gaudy jewels, carved figures, rubber daggers—and showmanship. It works beautifully—when set in motion, the daring marvel in tights and handlebar mustache dives headlong toward a tiny tank, and rings the bell at the bottom of his plunge. This creation, however, would not withstand even one sibling fight over whose turn it was.

Sally Wetherby, with her delicious sense of humor, does not spend all her waking hours gathering turned wood and reassembling it. Most of her days are filled with taxi service, Little League, cats and dogs and children, and household humdrum. Her funny, clever toys are

59, 60, 61 Tower of Thrills, 5' high. Man at top of tower (detail far right) dives between guide wires, past mirrored column into a tiny tank, ringing the bell. Painted doll figures installed in other tanks (detail at left) suggest previous divers. Perilous dive is completed between shiny points of upturned razor-sharp rubber knife blades. By Doug Hansen.

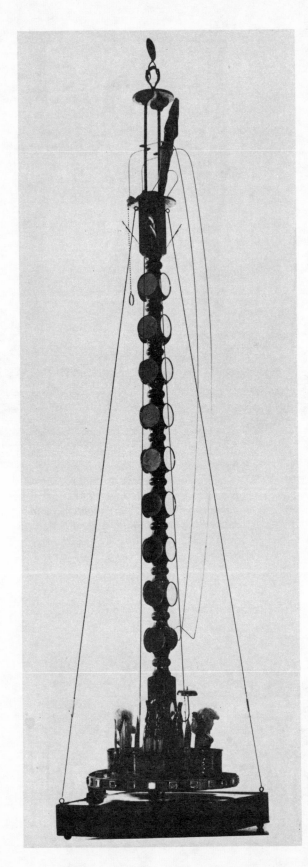

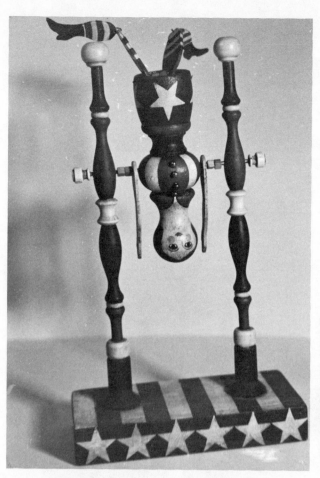

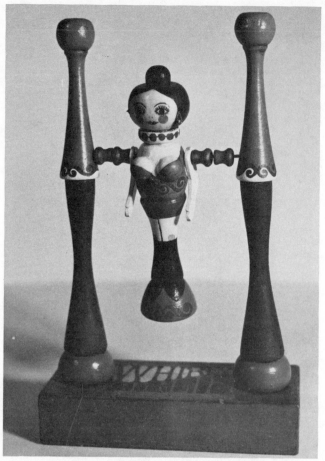

62 Tumbling Lady is an assemblage of turned pieces, richly painted and decorated. Designer cut arms and legs from thin craft plywood. By Sally Wetherby.

64 Lathe-turned figures of men, women, and children have strongly contrasting patterns of wood grain. The hardwood people suggest a chess set or other game figures. 2" to 7", by Arthur Lind.

63 Whirlie Girlie—the clever addition of details changes a piece of chair leg into a bosomy lady in high boots. The 9½" figure is painted with bright enamel and rubbed with raw umber. A good pat on the fanny sends her reeling.

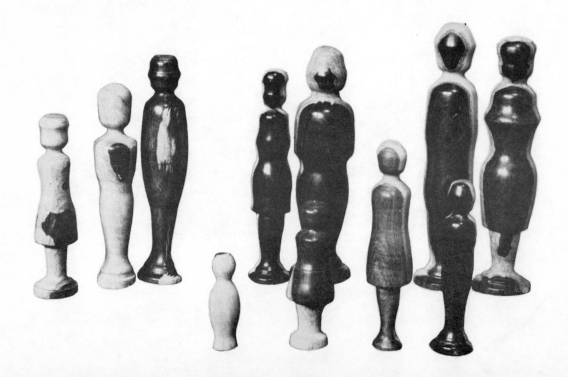

turned out in those occasional, scant hours left to her, and the toys are all the more incredible for it. The principal ingredient is small sections of turned wood combined with beads, dowels, scrap jewelry, and whatnot to create the figures shown in Plates 62, 63, 65 to 68. She makes what she needs and cannot find, such as faces, legs, and arms. There is nothing hit or miss about this work—if the balls don't make the balancing man balance, they get drilled and filled with melted lead until they work right. Even the wood bases are filled with plaster if needed for stability. After studying Color Plates 2 and 4 of Sally's playthings, we

65, 66 Unicycle Man is a sober-faced gay-nineties figure reeking of determination, spinning his wheel but going nowhere. He is made of found pieces of wood turnings with arms and legs added by the designer. 14",
by Sally Wetherby.

67 Man on a Stork. Enigmatic man in a
bowler hat sits astride a stork made of
assembled wood objects. Designer
Sally Wetherby painted the 10" figure with
bright enamel paint and antiqued it.

68 Assembled pieces of wood make a
convincing Strong Man with bulging
bead-muscles. Figure is painted with bright
enamel. 9" tall, by Sally Wetherby.

69 *Airplane Man of stuffed velvet,*
17", by Lenore Davis.

will all look at our buffet and chair legs with a different and calculating eye.

Silk screening is a method of printing many copies of the same thing, and is used for other toys in this book such as blocks and wheels. It is an ancient craft with materials and techniques of its own. With some modern and simplified variations, it is presently enjoying a vogue. If you want to use silk screen to make a few dozen of something, it is easy to find a good reference. The adult toy of Nixon and Kissinger in Plate 70 is made by a versatile craftsman who is a silk-screen teacher.

70 *Strange bedfellows are*
silk-screened arm in arm and stuffed
as one figure. Faces are
silk-screened from a newspaper
photo and stitched onto doll figure.
10", by Sandra Darnley.

The bodies are printed, cut out, and stuffed as one shape. The faces were made by photo silk-screen process, using a published photograph. The printed faces were then hand sewn to the body forms. RN is making his famous victory sign and Henry waves a small silk flag.

Lenore Davis, better known for her soft sculpture, has stuffed a toy for adults, people who have lived long enough to know what "earthbound" really means. Airplane Man, an aerodynamic wonder, makes graceful wing tips with his hands and achieves balanced flight without straightening his knees. He is shown in Plate 69 and Color Plate 32.

Quilt maker and designer Else Brown made the beautiful doll in Plates 71 and 72. A layer of light, sheer fabric is machine-stitched to a dark fabric backing. Areas to be accented are slit from the back and stuffed, a technique called trapunto. Additional depth comes from the dark layer showing through the light layer.

71, 72 Trapunto doll, 26", by quiltmaker Else Brown. Detail opposite.

73 Family portrait made from a 7″
by 9″ black-and-white photograph.
The photo was glued to a thin
piece of Masonite and sawed with
a jigsaw.

Puzzles

Jigsaw puzzles appeal to young and old. Few people can resist the intrigue of a half-finished puzzle. A permanent floating 500-piece puzzle set up on a card table is a place where all generations can participate as equals. Immediately after he passes the puzzle-eating stage, a child can be introduced to the rudiments of puzzle assembling. A grandpa no longer up to romping or piggybacking can teach the beginner the merits of finding all the straight-edge border pieces first and assembling them. A house guest who wouldn't have anything else to do with a small kid might introduce him to the fierce discipline of working his way uniformly across the puzzle the way a tomato worm consumes a plant.

Puzzles are one area of activity where a child's inexperience is readily compensated for by his energy and determination. Eager novices try ten possible pieces in one spot for every one considered by your experienced eye. Of course we must each make for ourselves the character-molding decision: Is it fair or not to study the picture on the box for aid in putting the pieces together?

Puzzles are much more fun when worked by groups rather than solo. They are portable, hence conveniently taken to a friend's house, or to the lake for the summer. They can be assembled in the toolshed when you don't dare show your face in the house. They are compatible with conversation—either end of it. If you want to spend a little time with a chatterbox, you can work on a puzzle together; if *you* are the chatterbox, resistance is less here than in playing bridge or watching TV.

Family photographs (see Plate 73), school pictures, prints, and magazine pictures can be used to make your own puzzles. Surely an old college roommate would enjoy receiving a picture puzzle of herself. And what child wouldn't delight in putting together the pieces of a puzzle showing him with last summer's big fish?

For a really satisfactory puzzle, the paper must stay adhered to the wood or hardboard (such as Masonite). Therefore, here are a few words of direction and advice. Gather the materials needed: puzzle picture, white glue, and hardboard. Use a stiff-bristled brush to "paint"

the glue onto the hardboard, then lay the picture in place and cover it with a protecting paper. Rub it with the flat of your hand until the air bubbles are out and the glue starts to set. Then cover it with a heavy object, such as an old year book, until the glue is completely dry. This last step is the secret of success for permanence in gluing paper to a heavy backing. For good results, the thinner the paper being adhered, the thinner the layer of glue should be. Greater perma-

74, 75 Rabbit and turtle puzzles are made from plywood or hardboard. After undercoating, paint the details of the animals; cut with a jigsaw or coping saw. By Jackie Vermeer.

nence can be achieved by lacquering the surface when the glue is dry or by "painting" with a final layer of white glue, which hardens to a clear shiny protective coat.

If you can draw well enough to suit yourself, make your own puzzle drawing directly on wood. Plates 74 and 75 show simple animal puzzles made from drawings. Saw out the parts, sand, and paint. Interlocking parts stay in place best (see Drawing 9) and are therefore

Drawing 9 Cut jigsaw puzzle in interlocking strips, then go back and cut strips between each two knobs, making a knob with each short cut.

76 Double-layer puzzle made from a six-year-old's drawing of a horse. Note saw line in lower right corner where the sawing began and ended. Bag in which to keep the puzzle completes the toy. 5" by 6", by Liz Laury.

more satisfactory than straight edges or slight curves. Plan to use interlocking, unless you decide to retain certain shapes in the photograph or picture part of your puzzle.

For younger children, a double-layer puzzle is more easily assembled. Start with two layers of wood or Masonite of the same size and set one aside as the backing of the puzzle. On the other piece, draw and saw the puzzle, leaving all or most of the outside edge intact for a border or frame. Glue this outside edge permanently to the back piece. Note in Plate 76, which shows a double-layer puzzle, that the horse rider's arm is too delicate a line to saw and was therefore permanently painted on the border surface. The puzzle in Plate 77 has a second picture painted on the backing surface which is exposed when the cut pieces are lifted out. Another example of this kind of puzzle is shown in Plate 78. Note in these examples how the sawing starts at the edge of the wood, goes around the figures and comes back out on the same line it entered. Paint the loose pieces and the edge as you would a single-layer puzzle.

Some thought should be given to the age and ability of the puzzle user when the puzzle is being made. The permanently framed puzzle (double layer) is a good one for beginners, with the frame forming a "pen" to help keep the pieces in place.

Interlocking parts are a good idea for all puzzles. A slight bump from one enthusiastic, rambunctious puzzle worker can set the whole project back several minutes and may evoke glares and harsh words from

77 *Puzzle on Masonite made from a child's drawing. When loose pieces are removed, another drawing painted on the back piece of Masonite is revealed. 7″ high.*

78 *Double-layer Masonite puzzle, with a bag made to fit and match it. 8″ wide.*

79, 80, 81 Commercial greeting cards form the basis of these puzzles.
Get-well card of bright bold design arrives as a toy for a sick child. Thick
plywood lets individual pieces or the entire puzzle stand upright. For most
pleasing results, avoid cutting across faces.

82 Toymaker Ruth Law neglects shopping and laundry to cut the block puzzle shown in the photo below.

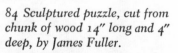

83 A complex puzzle in which the pieces are toys. All fit back together to form a block, 7″ by 8″.

84 Sculptured puzzle, cut from chunk of wood 14″ long and 4″ deep, by James Fuller.

other puzzle workers. The more pieces more intricately cut, the more complex the puzzle, of course. If you want to add to the fun, use two copies of the same magazine picture and adhere one copy to each side of the Masonite.

For interlocking sawing of the prepared pictures, decide how many pieces the finished puzzle is to have. Make the cuts each way according to the proportion of the uncut picture. For example, if you decide on a one hundred piece puzzle and the picture which forms the puzzle is about square, ten cuts each way is logical. If the puzzle is about twice as long as it is wide, make twice as many cuts the long way.

Any child (or adult) would find it more fun to receive a birthday or get-well card that was cut into a puzzle. Plate 79, a card about a new baby, is cut into a puzzle and can be put back in the envelope along with the message half. Plate 80 is a very bright glossy card so attractive anyone would want to assemble it, feeling better or not. It is made on ½″ plywood, so it will stand on edge when assembled. The puzzle in Plate 81 is so large (20″) that it takes some time to cut it apart, and longer for a child to put it back together. It was cut in such a way that the message can be discarded if it is not appropriate.

In addition to the usual use of the puzzle, games can be devised which are both challenging and amusing for children. For example, several commercially made identical greeting cards can be glued to wood and cut in pieces. No two will be cut in an identical manner, so the pieces will be similar, though only the right ones will fit. The game is to find the exact pieces that will fit the ones that you or your team have. This will work well for Christmas and Valentine cards.

For a finished effect, puzzles should come with a container for putting them away. A simple draw string bag can be made on the sewing machine in little time. Two such bags are shown in Plates 76 and 78. Or how about covering a box with a lid and keeping the puzzle in that? Hosiery boxes would be just about right if you had enough foresight to design your puzzle that size.

Drawing 10 Small board with drilled holes makes an interesting color puzzle for the very young. Paint square areas around each hole in different colors. Paint dowel pegs to match each of the squares.

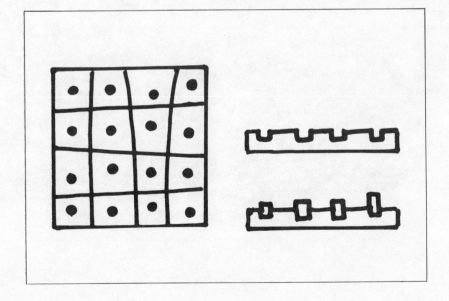

85 *A wise bird offers simple shapes to be batik decorated. 10″ high, by Kay Schneider.*

Stuffed Animals

Long before

"the gingham dog and the calico cat
side by side at the table sat"

children were bringing their toy companions to lunch. Animals, stuffed plump and soft, were taken to the table, to nap, to play, and (of course) to bed at night. Almost every child has a favorite—some tamed, domesticated fuzzy bear, rabbit, blanket, or dog without which sleep seems impossible.

Stuffed toys are surely the all-time, all-age favorite. The affection lavished on these animals is genuine and deep, and the attachments sometimes last far longer than the possessor may enjoy admitting. We all know of parents whose childhood favorites have survived to be enjoyed by their own children. This doesn't just happen. Only a well-loved animal gets set aside (not tossed out) when baseball bats or tennis rackets or a driver's license become the center of a young person's life. It is not too uncommon for a dormitory room or college apartment to be peopled with the slightly worn but comforting presence of these familiar and much-loved bears or lambs.

Many adults, who find that the names of best friends in kindergarten or of the girl next door have faded, recall vividly the favored stuffed animal. They are sometimes embarrassed to admit that the beloved toy is packed safely away in an attic trunk or tucked in with the children's toys. Much of this devotion must result from the fact that the toy belongs to the child in a way that a real animal, or a friend, or a brother can never belong to him. The child becomes responsible for it, and therein lies the attachment.

Today's children, like yesterday's, love a small bundle to hold and cuddle. These stuffed bundles are not only popular, but (fortunately) are the easiest of all toys to make. Regardless of your skills with tools or designs, a stuffed animal is not beyond your capacity. As far as that goes, children themselves produce some of the most delightful stuffed toys of all. Since stuffed animals are so appropriate for toddlers,

86 Brilliant yellow and orange
spots form the camouflage of this
batik giraffe by fabric artist
Elizabeth Fuller. The animal's
horns are 5½' above the ground.

Drawing 11 The simplest felt shapes, sewn together at the outside edge, offer the essential features of a bear. After sewing about ⅔ of the way around, insert stuffing.

Drawing 12 When cutting out shapes from woven material, such as wool, corduroy, or velveteen, allow an extra ¼″ for seams. Machine sew with right sides facing together; then turn, stuff, and close opening with a slip-stitch.

87 Batik teddy bear is made from two pieces of fabric on which a bear was drawn with wax. 12″ high, by Margaret "Mog" Miller.

those made for them must be safe. What is sewn on must *stay* on. The fabric and the stuffing should be washable.

If you are making your first stuffed toy, try a simple two-piece construction as shown in Drawing 11. When that is easily mastered, move on to a more complex one. The simple form allows for many kinds of decorative detail and for that reason is sometimes superior to the more complicated one. Also, there are fewer seams to come apart!

Plate 85 shows a simple two-piece construction for a bird which has been decorated with batik. This is a resist method of dyeing fabric in which a hot melted wax is painted onto the material. When the wax has cooled, the fabric is placed in a dye bath. Then the wax is removed, either with solvent or by ironing the wax between layers of paper towels. The waxed areas will have resisted the dye, leaving the original fabric color as the painted design. The process is repeated for each additional color.

Many of the stuffed toys in this chapter have been batiked. See Plates 85 through 92. Some designers paint the animal shapes directly on yardage, cutting out the animal from the batik later. Others prefer to cut the desired animal shape first, and then paint within that area. Many excellent references are available on the batik technique if you are interested in pursuing that special effect. Care must always be taken in heating the wax, so follow directions and take all precautions. If batik is already your thing, even the zoo is not your limit.

88 *This batik beast assumed his ferocious nature under Kay Schneider's paint brush. 24" long.*

89 *Stuffed batik lion has an elaborate mane. 20" high, by Margaret "Mog" Miller.*

The marvelous creature in Plate 88, though obviously a wild beast, has very friendly intentions. Batik artist Kay Schneider created him and his companion bird in Plate 85. The beast is seen in full camouflage in Color Plate 49. "Mog" Miller's gentle animals in Plates 89, 90, and 91 are softly colored batik fabrics, lightly stuffed with polyester batting. Her angel is shown in Color Plate 48.

An almost life-size giraffe by Elizabeth Fuller received his spots from Elizabeth's batik brush. See Plate 86. She draws the outlines for her animals on fabrics, then paints the wax designs. When the batik process is finished, the parts are cut out, then sewn together. Elizabeth used wood framework for the construction of the legs and neck, which

90 Tiger was drawn and painted on cotton fabric, then cut out and sewn. 15" high, by Margaret "Mog" Miller.

91 Butterfly, with a 16″ wing span,
by Margaret "Mog" Miller.

92 A reclining ram, 6″ high, is
batik on heavy cotton fabric,
by Elizabeth Fuller.

she then padded and filled. Used cotton sheets provided fabric for the giraffe—sheets offer large areas of fabric on which to work, and the undyed cottons are excellent for some batik dyes. The giraffe is stuffed with wadded paper, which works well under a fairly sturdy cotton such as this. The paper stuffing lasts longer and works better than might be supposed. The ram in Plate 92 is an additional example of Elizabeth Fuller's batik. It is filled with cotton batting.

93 Fuzzy wool made a soft base fabric for an embroidered bear, 8″ tall, by Marlo Johansen.

94 Animal bean bags, from fake fur, are stuffed with dried beans or popcorn (unpopped, please!). 8″ high, by Jackie Vermeer and Marian Lariviere.

95 A collection of old blue jeans was cut and sewn into a bear by Lilo Nassé. 21" high.

96 A velveteen bear, made like the one of blue jeans, by Lilo Nassé.

97 These sober-looking bears are silk-screened on felt, then cut and machine sewn. By varying the colors of paint as well as felt, the bears take on different personalities. 12" high, by Jean Ray Laury.

98 Kittens with a mother cat, designed and sewn by nine-year-old Hilary Jean Law. 3" high.

The teddy bear is among the most loved of all animals. The short arms and legs give it a compact shape, easy to carry and hold. Many adults have found a teddy bear acceptable for a boy, while they tremble at the mere thought of his playing with a doll. Boys have probably been denied a lot of companionship due to this overconcern for their masculinity. (Boys *do* become parents.) But we've discussed dolls in another chapter—we are now on the trail of bear.

By cutting two identical shapes, one for the front and one for the back, the bear (or any other animal) can be formed and features added by various techniques. A very simple bear form is illustrated in Drawing 11. One outline shape is all that is needed. Whatever is added beyond that is up to the interests and skills of the crafter. The bear could be cut from felt and sewn on the top side. If it is cut from fur or fake fur, or a woven fabric, it should be sewn with right sides together, then turned. See Drawing 12.

All two-piece stuffed animals can be made in this way. More complex animals may use this same approach to form the individual parts of an animal. For example, arms and legs can be made separately, sewn, turned and stuffed. Then those limbs can be inserted into the seams of the body. See Drawing 14.

Drawing 13 Three-piece animals will stand upright. First join the two identical body pieces, then add a third base piece by stitching it into the opening.

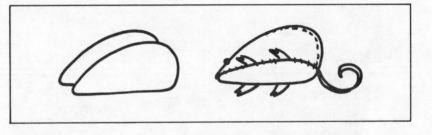

Drawing 14 Parts of animals can be sewn and stuffed separately. They are then inserted between the layers of the main body.

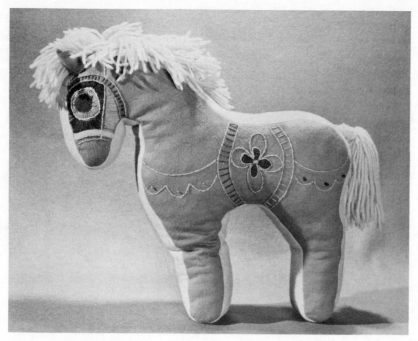

99 Embroidery enlivens the plump
horse made from felt, using two
profile pieces with a long strip to
join them. 17″ high,
by Helen Rene Bonner.

100 Perching bird uses two pieces
of felt for the sides; a third piece
forms the base or underneath side.
6″ long, by Mark Law.

Drawing 15 A button strung
between the body and legs of an
animal serves as a bearing to let
parts move freely.

101 *The movable legs of a jointed fabric horse, 8" high, can be set at a gallop, canter, or pace. By Char Aidan.*

102 *An elegant, dignified horse was made by high school student and horse lover Betsy McLeod. It is 7" high, uses appliqué of nylon mesh stockings over a padded wire armature.*

103 A young snake charmer mimics the wide-mouthed knitted viper . . .

104 peers into the knitted tubular interior; plunges a hand inside, and . . .

105 rescues a mouse, whose tail escapes through her fingers. The snake, over 6' long, hatched out of Gayle Smalley's knitting basket.

1. *Lulu Doll, 24" tall,*
   by Gloria McNutt

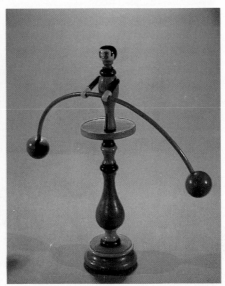

2. *Patriotic Lady, 13" tall,*
   by Sally Wetherby

3. *Dragon, 10" tall,*
   by Jane Cadman

4. *Balancing Man, 17",*
   by Sally Wetherby

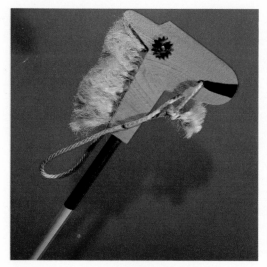

5. *Hobbyhorse, 4',
    by David Gordon*

6. *Lady Godiva, 10",
    by Jean Ray Laury*

7. *Clay Horse, 8",
    by Liz Laury*

8. *Horse Costume, Marin
    Renaissance Faire*

9. Trojan Horse, 12",
   by Ruth Law

10. Clothespin Knight, 5",
    by Ruth Law

11. Coldstream Guard, 26",
    by Gloria McNutt

12. *Quaker Puffed Liberty, 22",*
    by Susan Morrison

13. *Neighbor, 15",*
    by Jean Ray Laury

14. *Elephant in the Flower Bed,*
    4", by Ruth Law

15. *Three Wise Men, 5", by Ruth Law*

16. *Circus Cage, 8", by Ruth Law*

17. *Hippie Doll, 12″,*
by Bets Barnard

18. *Red Head, 12″,*
by Jean Ray Laury

19. *Doll, 11″, by Bets Barnard*

20.   *Old Woman in the Shoe, 7", by Ruth Law*

21.   Rag Dolls, 16" to 20", by Ruth Law

22.   Hobbyhorse, 15",
       by Susan Morrison

23.   Herd of Hobbyhorses,
       by Susan Morrison

In Plate 93, a very simple bear is made elegant with yarn embroidery which adds color, texture, and pattern. The stout and solidly stuffed teddy bears of blue jeans and velveteens in Plates 95 and 96 are very popular with youngsters who come to visit.

The bears in Plate 97, again a simple outline, have been printed with the silk-screen process. This two-piece form can be used for almost any animal. The cats in Plate 98 and most of the batik animals already shown are examples of this two-piece approach.

A two-piece animal usually does not stand up. You need at least three pieces to accomplish this—one way is to add this third section at the bottom, as for the mouse in Drawing 13. In working out your pattern, you may find it easier to cut and sew the animal side shapes first, then cut the third shape to fit the opening. The bird in Plate 100, a three-piece form, is sewn in this way. Because it is a top-sewn felt you can easily see how it is joined.

The process used to assemble the horse in Plate 99 is an extension of the two-piece animal. Helen Bonner cut two identical horse shapes, then joined them with a 4″ strip of felt between. This is a speedy, simple, and very effective way to produce a three-dimensional form. Be sure to align the two side pieces when they are joined to the flat shape. Embroidery is most easily done before the seams are sewn. Mane and tail are added after stuffing is complete.

Stuffed toys can also be built up using a more sculptural approach. The horse in Plate 102 was padded and stitched over a wire armature. Betsy McLeod created the beautiful animal with an appliqué patchwork of nylon mesh over the padded armature. Coat-hanger wire or baling wire can be bent and shaped easily with pliers; padding is wrapped and stitched over the wire before the final layer of nylon is added. Color Plate 3 shows a magnificent dragon created by another high school student.

106 With a chain-stitch smile, this soft knitted kitten enjoys her rest. 16″, by Becky Hansen.

To make a jointed animal, the legs must be made separate from the body. The completed parts can be assembled by using a cord or string pulled all the way through the legs as well as the body. In Plate 101 the cord is tied at the ends. Sometimes a button or washer is used between the body and the leg to make the movement smoother. See Drawing 15. A button or bead at the outside of the leg may make tying easier. If two strings or cords are run through the button at one time, it will be simple to tie them together. The process is similar to adding wheels to a toy car body. Think of the connecting string as a flexible axle.

Knitting and crochet offer great flexibility for forming animals. Gayle Smalley knitted the relaxed serpent in Plate 103. The knitting stitch varies from top to bottom so that the snake's underside has markings that are distinct from the top. She keeps the hollow tubular

107 An exhausted horse rests on his crocheted posterior. It stands about three hands high. By Alison Law, who learned to crochet by making this animal when she was ten.

108 A knitted lion has mane and tail of yarn. 6″ high, by Jan Voight.

66

109 Feelie Beast combines
knitting, stuffing, appliqué and
embroidery. 17" high,
by Sachi Honmyo.

110 Fabric serpent, stuffed and
jointed, flicks a bright red tongue.
4½" long, by Jude Martin.

111 Old-time favorites,
the Rockford work-sox
monkeys, appear in many
variations and seldom are
two alike. 20",
by Vella Draughn and
Lydia Bitters.

opening of the mouth filled with small stuffed mice and birds. The viper is a little too realistic for many adults, but children love plunging their hands into the mouth to rescue small creatures. The gesture is not unlike that of the woodsman rescuing Red Riding Hood's grandmother from the wolf . . . or the three pigs from inside another notorious wolf.

Becky Hansen knitted the soft squeezable stuffed kitten in Plate 106. The Chessy-cat grin is added with a chain stitch in yarn. A horse, in the pose typical of the story book favorite Eyeore, was the first crochet effort of ten-year-old Alison Law. Figuring out how as she went along, she created this delightful favorite, then stuffed him with fabric scraps matching the color of the yarn. See Plate 107.

Mice, always a favorite of children, can be made over a simple armature of pipe cleaners, as shown in Plates 114 and 115. The mice in Plate 116 are made of felt—the rolled felt forming the body is stiff enough to let them stand upright.

Even more complex-looking animals may be figured out easily if you do the body shape separately from the legs. Mice, mole, frog, and turtle in Plates 112, 117 to 120 are joined in this way.

More animals by a very young toymaker are shown in Plates 121

112 Stuffed mice have patterned ears and braided tails, along with appliquéd eyes. 5" long, by Jude Martin.

113 Circular patterns in crochet form a rabbit, with face and ears finished in appliqué. 14" to the tip of his ears. Designer unknown.

114 Mice, dancing the stately
minuet.
By Wendy and Nancy Northup.

115 Pipe cleaners form the body of
a delightful mouse. Head is
stitched felt. 4" high,
by Wendy and Nancy Northup.

116 Country mouse family of felt
by Alison Law at age eleven. 3" to
4" tall (the mice, not Alison).

117 A wary 10″ turtle, from woolen yardage, was pieced and stuffed by Jude Martin.

118 Plaid wool emphasizes the mouth and under sides of a worried-looking frog. 9″, by Jude Martin.

119 A huggable pig, 9″ long, by Chris LeCoq.

120 Mole, out in the daylight, reveals his fake fur, felt, and dotted swiss costume. 9″ long with an 18″ tail, by Chris LeCoq.

121 A magnificent hippo resulted from twelve-year-old Alison Law's first efforts with sewing machine. 18″ long.

122 (Below right) Children are not intimidated by even the most difficult sounding projects. Here a kangaroo baby peers from the pouch where he was sewn by Alison Law.

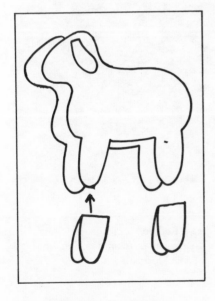

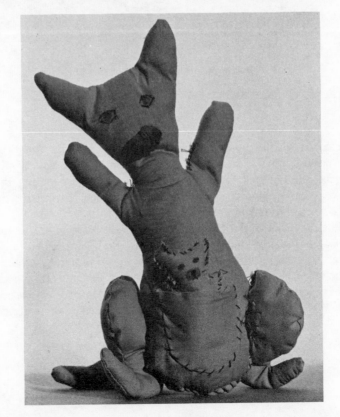

Drawing 16 A more complex animal grows out of the basic two-piece approach. Ears are added, and additional leg pieces turn the original two-legged animal into a four-legged one.

and 122. In the first, Alison figured out a way to use the two-piece body, adding four legs. She did this by cutting as you would any two-piece animal, then inserting a strip to go across, joining the two front legs and providing the underneath of each. Another strip was used to form the back legs. See Drawing 16.

While real or fake furs are always appropriate for stuffed toys, printed fabrics offer the advantage of rich patterns and smooth textures. Plates 124 and 125 show examples of the very lively complex surfaces that were achieved through this combination by Lenore Schwartz Goodell.

The superlative hippopotamus shown in Plate 123 is Susan Morrison's Lady on a Hippo. Nearly 3' long, this sculptured fabric beast

123 *Lady on a Hippo*, 32" long, created by artist and dollmaker Susan Morrison.

124 A multi-patterned creature,
obviously emerging from the sea,
is a Lenore Schwartz Goodell
design.

125 A magnificent many-legged
lizard, 16" long, was created
by Lenore Schwartz Goodell.

126, 127 *Swallowing his prey whole, the Super Slug stretches out to a length of 10'. The boy-lunch, crawling on all fours, emerges at the other end! Super Slug's stuffed teeth and furry eyelashes* (opposite) *add to the tactile pleasures of being swallowed alive. By Joyce Bossom Parmeter.*

is stitched, padded, and appliquéd in a variety of irresistible textures and rich colors. Susan's skill, wit, and imagination are equally evident in Fred and Mildred Go to the Prom. See Color Plate 33.

An animal on a grand scale is the Super Slug by Joyce Bossom Parmeter in Plates 126 and 127. Fake fur and upholstery fabrics cover the basic structure, which is a sauna tube (the type used for pouring concrete columns). She drilled holes in the tube in order to sew the fabric securely to it. The slug's blue eyelids are fringed with real fur. Braving the giant teeth, children crawl in the 10' long tunnel and emerge through the curtain of tail feathers. Made for an exhibition, thousands of children crawled through and literally wore him out.

128 Sturdy rocking horse, made
from 2 by 4's with peg
construction. 2' high,
by Charles Nassé.

4 More Animals

Less cuddly than their stuffed counterparts but more suitable for outdoor play are animals made from wood, cardboard, mâché, or clay. Some may be sat on or climbed over—others are moved or manipulated. The range is wide, from the simplest suggestion of an animal to the more complex and detailed forms. Much of the job in making these toys is in their larger scale and permanence.

The rider in Plate 128 has put many miles on his tireless steed. The construction is of special interest, with overlapping and pegged joints. The rocker itself is reinforced with a curved board, adding strength and a foot rest to serve as stirrups.

Cut plywood, sanded and painted, was used for a simple hobby-horse in Plate 129. Leather thong reins and cotton-ball-fringe mane complete the details. To attach the head firmly, a 1" dowel was slotted as shown in Drawing 18. The width of the slot should be the same thickness as the wood used for the head, to get a tight fit. It is then glued and pegged.

Susan Morrison's elegant riding-stick hobbyhorses (Color Plates 22 and 23) are more than show horses—they get their share of being patted, galloped, hugged, abandoned, and loved. Susan has pieced, stuffed, padded, embroidered, and embellished them to a point of pure visual and tactile delight, as evidenced in Plate 130.

If these elegant hobbyhorses seem beyond your competence, try making a simple, lovable old nag. Old sox may be used as the base for a horse head. See Drawing 17 and Color Plate 5. A horse of a different breed is shown in Color Plate 7.

Cora Pahl's magnificent pulp-mâché animals, Plates 131 through 134, are grand in scale and disarmingly personal.

With feet firmly planted, the hippopotamus in Plate 133 is a marvelous near-sighted creature of pulp-mâché. An armature or frame of expandable steel was built first, then padded with pulp mixed with water. After the surface is sanded to smoothness, it is painted and decorated with acrylic or enamel paints. Leather ears give a textural change, as do glass eyes that peer out from the lotus blossoms painted

129 Painted head of a simple
plywood hobbyhorse is set into a
slotted dowel. By Ruth Law.

130 A rider nuzzles the full yarn
mane of a stuffed fabric
hobbyhorse. By Susan Morrison.

131 Pulp-mâché rocking horse was
built over a wood armature, making
the animal sturdy enough for
rocking horse enthusiasts of all
ages. 35" tall, by Cora Pahl.

Drawing 17 (Above) The work-sock hobbyhorse is an old favorite. A toe becomes the horse's nose, and the entire sock is stuffed and tied to a portion of broom stick. Mouths are added by slitting the end of the sock on the mouth line, then inserting an extra piece of fabric.

Drawing 18 (Right) To attach a plywood hobbyhorse head to a dowel or stick, the stick may be slotted. The slot should be the same width as the thickness of the head.

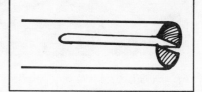

132 With feet firmly planted on barrel staves, Cora Pahl's elaborately painted pachyderm awaits its mahout. 20″ high.

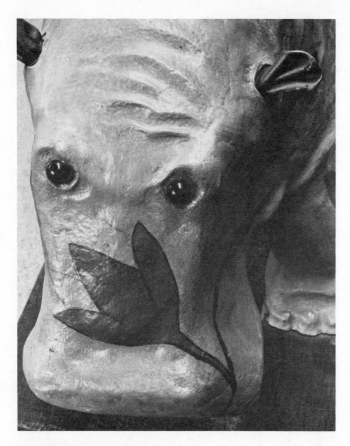

133 Detail. A lotus blossom curls around the nose of a glassy-eyed hippo.

134 A magnificent hippo, 27" high, rocks on his barrel-stave platform. A paper pulp-mâché process was used by artist Cora Pahl to produce the wide-eyed animal of the rivers.

135 (Left) Strips of newspaper cover a simple armature of cardboard tubes and masking tape to form this dog. It is strong enough for a child to sit on. Head to toe is 22". By Liz Laury at age ten.

136 (Opposite) A massive ceramic horse, fired but unglazed, makes a permanent and durable mount for as many as four children at one time. 40" tall, by Stan Bitters.

on the hippo's blue skin. The animal is finally attached to wood staves which allow him to rock gently amid his flowers.

Another of Cora Pahl's animals is the rocking horse in Plate 131. It is similarly structured and obviously intrigues grown-ups who like to play, as well as children.

The papier-mâché dog in Plate 135, made by a ten-year-old, is sturdy and stable. Four cardboard tubes (from paper toweling) attached to a 1″ board with masking tape, provided a structure for the legs and back. Cardboard boxes were taped to this for the neck and the head. See Drawing 19. Newspaper strips are dipped into a liquid wheat paste (or wallpaper paste) and wrapped around the entire body. Use several layers of these strips, then let them dry. To shape some areas, such as the rib cage, tape wadded newspapers onto the body and add more strips. The more strips of pasted paper, the stronger the form will be when dry. Because the paper dries hard and strong, this 2′ animal can be sat on. When the final shape is finished, allow the paper to dry thoroughly. It then can be painted or finished with a final layer of colored paper or cloth.

Another papier-mâché animal by the same young toymaker is shown in Plate 137. Also formed from cardboard tubes, the finished giraffe was decorated with poster paints (or tempera), then coated with a plastic varnish.

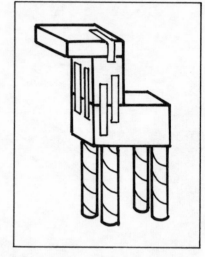

Drawing 19 Cardboard boxes and tubes, taped together, offer a basic structure to which papier-mâché strips can be added.

137 Papier-mâché giraffe, painted with poster paints, has a finishing coat for permanence. 12″ high, by a ten-year-old.

138 A half-finished horse shows the masking tape over newspaper with the outer surface partially covered by pulp-mâché. 7″ high, by Liz Laury at age eleven.

There are papier-mâché mixes that come by the bag. These are shredded paper, ready-mixed with paste, to which you add water. This makes a pulp that can be formed in the hands like clay. In Plate 138, an animal base was made from small rolls or tubes of newspaper held in place with masking tape. The pulp-mâché is padded onto the frame of the animal. Successive layers can be added until the final shape is achieved.

Anyone with access to clay and a kiln can make toys that are truly permanent. One large-scale piece is shown in Plate 136. The horse, constructed by the "pinch" method, was left hollow. (It was fired to cone 04.) Theoretically, it is breakable, but this one has withstood twelve years of backyard play, numerous moves, and has been known to hold four or five children at one time. The piece is extremely heavy, which gives it the stability needed for being climbed on. What it lacks in mobility it makes up in sturdiness.

Almost every child responds with enthusiasm to the pliable possibilities of clay. Many schools have kilns for firing children's works. If none is available to you, most commercial ceramic studios of the hobby-shop variety will fire your clay, charging by size. Plates 139 through 141 show clay animals made by children.

139, 140, 141 Clay is a medium to which children readily respond. The little horse, kitty, and elephant were each shaped in minutes by an eight-year-old girl.

142 Whale and fish were drawn on wood by a six-year-old and sawed from ½″ pine. 3″ long.

143 Whale, 4″ long, was drawn and sawed out by a four-year-old.

144 Crayon drawing on paper can be glued to hardboard, then sawed out. Children love to play with animals of their own making.

145 Cats, drawn with marking pen on wood, become three-dimensional animals as they emerge from the ½″ pine. 3″, by Alison Law.

146, 147, 148 *A child's drawing of a Bactrian camel and an elephant, too intriguing to pass by, were sawed out of wood and painted by an adult. Cutout ears and painted daisies are added to simplest basic pig shape. Animals are 4" to 6" tall.*

One of the most direct methods of making animal forms is by cutting silhouettes or outlines from wood. It is not at all unlike cutting paper dolls, or paper animals, though these are three dimensional. The sea creatures in Plate 142 were drawn directly on wood by a six-year-old and cut from ½" pine by a parent. The durability of any decorative work added to the surface depends upon the coloring used and the final finish. Marking pens are great for children to use—colorful and fast. Some marking pens are not permanent color, however, and if used, the toy should be coated with a varnish or plastic spray, unless you are willing to have the color run when animals are left out overnight to graze in the foggy foggy dew. Gluing colored tissue papers to the surface adds color quickly. It can be sprayed for permanence.

The animals in Plate 144 are decorated with crayons. These were drawn on paper, the paper was then glued to Masonite, then the animals were sawed out. Plate 145 shows Alison Law's cats.

The elephant and Bactrian camel were drawn by a child, sawed and finished by an adult. Bright-colored enamels were used for the painted details. The pig is just as simple an animal, but the addition of ears, glued at each side, give it a more dimensional appearance. See Plates 146–48. Color Plates 9 and 14 show some superb painted-wood animals. An adult toymaker who finds animals difficult to draw can get the help of any child. He will be able to turn out drawings of his favorite animals faster than you can saw them. Toymakers too young to saw will find that adults enjoy cutting out their animal creations. So the possibilities for toymakers (young and old) working together are unlimited.

Woods can be left natural. In fact, the grain of unpainted wood can add interest to a toy, as in Plate 150. The unicorns, however, are made for an older child or for an adult. Though the horns and ears are of soft wood, it would not be safe for a toddler to carry these animals about. Another cluster of natural-wood toys is shown in Plate 152.

A wood animal made from a pecan is shown in Plate 151. An opening cut into the end of the pecan is closed with a small whittled plug of wood. The eyes and ears are light weight and move easily in their openings. To animate the pecan pig, catch a live fly and put it inside the pig (through the plug at the end). As the fly buzzes around, it moves the ears and eyes of the animal. The principle is the same as that which moves the Mexican jumping beans.

149 *Brightly painted and decorated animals were cut from one 1" pine board. 4" high, by Jerri Peters and Marlo Johansen.*

150 *Unicorns in the garden, 4″*
high, by Richard Graybill.

151 *Pecan pigs, a little over 1″*
high, have parts which move when
a live fly is given temporary
quarters inside.

The toymaker-sculptor will find few limitations for his talents when he applies his skills to wood. The possibilities with lamination, sawed wood, and carving can be seen throughout this book and in the magnificent Wild, Wild West Ride shown in Plate 153. It is an animal toy more for an adult's play than for a child's, though it is sturdy enough to withstand vigorous cranking.

The toy is animated by the handle in the center. This turning motion sends the horse up and down at a wild, wild gallop. The rider, only loosely attached to the saddle, flops violently back and forth with arms swinging. While the horse and rider gallop madly, the background scenery moves. A large disc, inside the box structure of the toy, has a continuous landscape scene. This disc is also turned by the handle, so the scenery flies by, making it beyond any doubt the wildest ride in the West.

152 A charming collection of simple forms, tapered at the ends to accent the head shapes, are sanded and left natural. 2½″ to 8″ high, by Arthur Lind.

153 *The Wild, Wild West Ride goes into frantic action when the handle at center is cranked. 26″ high, by Doug Hansen.*

154 *Detail, showing the carved balsa figure and horse.*

Swings, Strings, Springs

155 *Traditional two-rope swing of 1″ by 6″ pine plank. 20″ long, by Jackie Vermeer.*

156 *(Opposite) Roger Dupzyk's swing uses a large section of tree branch. A seat is added, and the swing is notched at the top for a rope. The swing was sanded, then varnished to finish and protect it from the weather. Courtesy of California Design X.*

String, cord, yarn, and rope are useful parts of many toys, beginning perhaps with the cat's cradle. The cat's cradle has intrigued scholars (as well as children) for centuries. It involves the manipulation of string looped around fingers and hands to form an infinite variety of designs and shapes as it passes from person to person. This toy is nothing more than a piece of string and two or more pairs of hands. This same piece of string, along with thread, cord, yarn, and rope, can be an essential and animating part of many toys.

A swing is one of the most popular toys requiring rope. One of its great virtues is that the user is an active participant, not a passive observer. Swings can be very simple or more versatile and complex. Anything you can ride on that is hung with one or more ropes is a swing, the chandelier notwithstanding. The great Tarzan himself may have given the first modern-day commercial for swings, hollering as he sailed through the air on that incredible grapevine.

Roger Dupzyk has built what is surely the most inviting swing ever. Starting with a huge naturally cured section of cedar (Plate 156), he carved a foot rest and added a seat. The pieces are shaped to fit together and are secured with glue and dowels. There are no nails or screws. The swing is suspended on its rope in the same manner a bow is strung. Without a rider, the swing lifts easily off the rope. The greater the weight put on it, the more tightly the rope is drawn around the wood. The wood is sanded smooth and sealed against weathering.

An old favorite is the drilled or notched board (Plate 155) hung on two ropes or one continuous rope. The board must have width and length enough to make a comfortable seat and be thick enough to support the weight of one or two children. A hole of sufficient diameter to accommodate the rope is drilled at each end, and the rope is pulled through to be knotted on the underside. The swing will hang outside in all kinds of weather. For this reason, the wood should be sealed to protect the surface and prevent splintering.

The circular, single-rope swing is easy to make and easy to ride (Plates 157, 158). Children find it more comfortable than do adults. It is a 7″ to 9″ circle of thick, exterior plywood, with a rope hole drilled

157, 158 (Opposite and above)
Single rope round swing made of
¾" exterior plywood, by Ruth Law.

159 (Right) Tub Swing from a
20" square, galvanized metal
container, by Ruth Law.

at the center. Plywood must be weatherproofed to prevent deterioration. Climb the tree first and attach the rope, then slip the disc on at the ground end, putting a double knot on the underside. While you are up in the tree quivering with fear, survey the area below to be sure the location allows clear movement in all directions; this swing can go around in circles.

If the swinger at your house thinks he's been everywhere and done everything in swings, try making a swing from an old galvanized tub. Drill four holes just under the top rim equidistant from each other and put in metal lap links for attaching the rope. (Lap links are like chain links but are open on one end. After they are installed, they can be hammered shut.) These four ropes must come together and be secured at

160 Spool Tractor—a rubber band provides the power.

161 A cotton rope is cut to correct length for jumper and delightfully finished with stuffed, life-sized hands for handles, by Jeri Barricklow.

162 Wire sculpture tricycle has a crank that winds up the rubber band. Trike is propelled forward in one brief, crazy little ride (or backward, if you turned the crank the wrong way). 5″ high, by H. O'Mura.

163 Buzz-button is a spinning toy made from a 3″ Masonite disc.

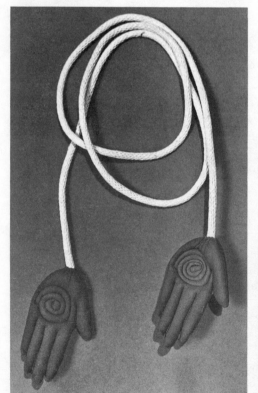

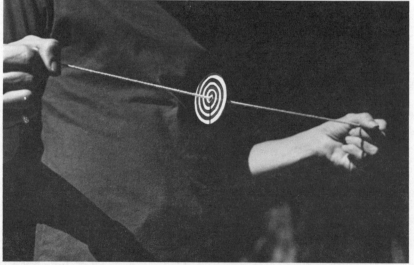

Drawing 20 Buzz-button, a cousin of the yo-yo, is an hypnotic toy that is easily assembled.

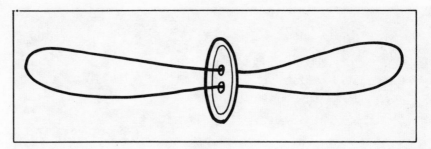

Drawing 21 Handles make pulling on ends easier.

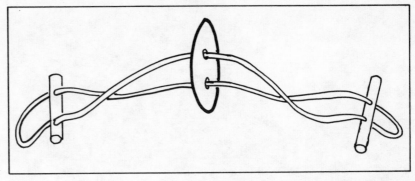

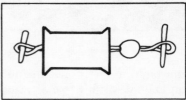

164, 165, 166 Girl and old man are made from cigarette boxes fastened to sticks. Hinged top of box forms lower jaw of talking figures. String running down along stick opens mouth; rubber band fastened inside box closes it. By Jackie Vermeer.

Drawing 22 Large wood matches, a bead, a spool, and a strong rubber band are all that are needed for "spool tractors."

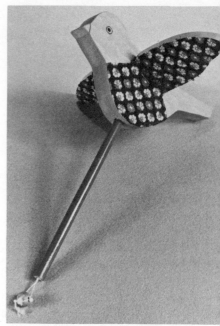

167, 168 *Hold bird by handle, pull bead on end of string threaded through hollow handle, and bird flaps its wings; release bead and wings drop down. 10" wingspan, by Ruth Law.*

one point so they can be tied to a single rope overhead. Plate 159 shows an example of this type of swing—made from a square tub instead of a round one.

Then there is the bag swing. Many a gunnysack came to its threadbare end stuffed with rags or straw and hung by a single rope from a tree. A burlap bag is not the best material for this type of swing, because it is loosely woven and eventually pulls apart. A stronger cloth, such as heavy denim or canvas, is preferable. Don't stuff the bag too full, and be sure to tie it tightly. Years ago an Iowa family had a great bag swing hung near the Sioux River. The rider pulled the swing back to a sawhorse, jumped on, then at the other end of the arc, let go and plunged into the river.

For the beginning swingmaker, here are a few helpful suggestions:

1. Hang your swing from a strong tree branch or beam. Remember that a two-rope swing moves in an arc in one plane; a one-rope swing may move in a circle like an inverted funnel. If the swing is to be hung from a beam, install a large eye bolt to which the rope can be tied. These bolts are available at the lumberyard.
2. Wherever the upper end of the rope is attached, be sure to tie it so that the rope does not slide back and forth or turn on the branch, because friction will cause the rope to fray and break eventually.
3. Several kinds of ropes are available and suitable for hanging swings. Make a few inquiries to help you determine which kind and size is best for the swing you have in mind.

Ranking in popularity with the swing is the jump rope. Children jump and skip over anything they can swing over their heads in an arc.

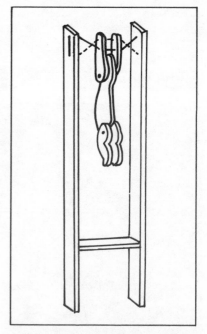

Drawing 23 Note string assembly for acrobatic figure. Crossbar must be free to "wobble" when toy is held and squeezed at bottom.

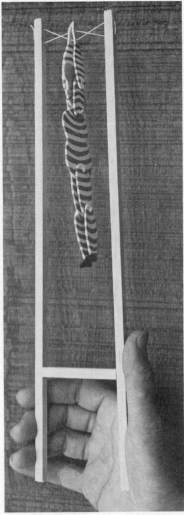

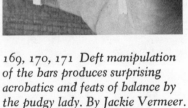

169, 170, 171 Deft manipulation of the bars produces surprising acrobatics and feats of balance by the pudgy lady. By Jackie Vermeer.

The flower garlands shown in paintings or the beribboned jumping ropes of May Day celebrations may be festive, but allow less mileage than those made of rope. Plate 161 shows a one-person jump rope of braided cotton rope—with hands for handles. The hands are made of stretch-knit fabric, stuffed, then stitched in the center to hold the inserted rope. These hands, about 5″ long, make good grips for the jumper.

A rubber band provides the power for the wire tricycle in Plate 162. Bending soft wire into figures and objects using only the hands or perhaps a pair of pliers is an absorbing occupation. The simple way to make a moving part is to hang one bent wire over another, but this tricycle goes considerably further; the axle is continuous with one rear wheel, and extends beyond the other wheel in the shape of a crank. The rubber band is looped onto the rear axle and stretched over the front fork of the trike. After the rubber band is wound, the unwinding action turns the wheels for a quick, giddy little trip. Seeing such a toy in action suggests other possible toys and other possible actions with a wound rubber band.

The buzz-button has been made in many shapes, but the action is essentially the same for all of them. A large button is strung on heavy thread or string as shown in Drawings 20 and 21. The ends of the string are held in each hand with the button suspended between as shown in Plate 163.

Wood spools are fast disappearing from the thread counters; Plate 160 shows an amusing toy made from an empty wood spool. This spool-tractor is powered by a wound-up rubber band installed in the spindle hole of the spool. Notches may be cut in the spool wheels (Drawing 22) for better traction and more noise.

A toymaker with a special interest in string-activated movement in toys should look at museum pieces or photographs of any Northwest Indian masks he can find. The Kwakiutl Indians in particular had a rich ceremonial life utilizing costumes and masks and hand-held objects, many of which had movable parts activated by pulled strings. The skill with which these Indians carved the indigenous wood compounds the interest these objects hold for craftsmen/toymakers.

A humble throw-away cigarette box forms the basic structure of the hand-held, string-activated talking toys in Plates 164 through 166. The basic structure is the box mounted on a paint stick. The flip-top is the lower jaw, which opens and closes with a string and a rubber band.

The flying birds of Plates 167, 168 are string-activated toys. The handle is a length of hollow cane such as nurserymen use to support plants. A double string goes up through the cane handle and the bird's body. One strand goes down through a hole in each wing. The string end is secured on the underside of the wing before the fabric hinge is glued into place. Pulling the bead makes the bird's wings flap.

The determined lady gymnast of Plates 169 through 171 is also string-activated. She is painted into her sweatsuit and assembled with knotted strings for maximum flexibility. The assembly of hands and string on the ends of the long bars is identical to that of the buzz-button. Alternately squeezing and releasing the bars below the flexible crossbar (Drawing 23) throws the lady head over heels over the string, and back. She can do half-nelsons, half-Immelmanns, mid-air somersaults, and chin-ups.

A jack-in-the-box is a figure constructed over a coiled metal spring. It is tucked into a box in such a way that it springs out when the box is opened. Plate 172 shows the exterior of an exceptionally well-made box with a wood and leather lid opener and metal hinges on the outside. In Plate 173 we can see the miter construction of the box and lid as well as the elaborate medieval jester whose grotesque papier-mâché head pops out. Notice the interior leather hinges which keep the lid from opening too far and help close the lid when the figure is pushed back into the box.

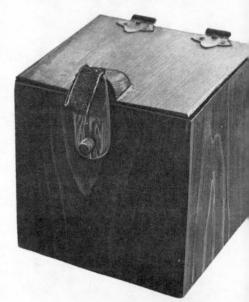

172, 173 Cloth-and-papier-mâché jack jumps out of heavy wood box made with double set of hinges and wood-and-leather lid-opening mechanism. 6" cube, by Terrie Sullivan Floyd.

174 Jenny-in-the-box is made from commercial jack-in-box with jack removed. Turn crank and out pops sassy Jenny made from a batting-stuffed nylon stocking. 6" high, by Jean Ray Laury.

Jenny-in-the-box in Plate 174 pops her insolent head out of a discarded commercially made jack box from a junk shop. When the cranked-out music reaches the critical point, it trips the lid and Jenny pops out. This box is covered with bright-colored felt glued onto the metal surface. Jenny is a piece of nylon stocking stuffed with batting. The facial features are shaped by pulling stitches to achieve the desired contours. (For more examples of nylon and batting heads, see Chapter I.) Coil spring of the original jack in this box pops her out.

175 *Sturdy, handsomely
constructed dump truck holds
back-seat driver. 24" long,
by Doug Parmeter.*

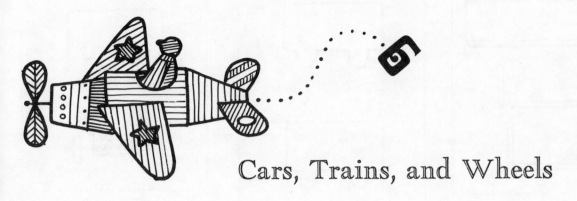

Cars, Trains, and Wheels

In the British Museum there is a two-wheeled toy found in a tomb on Cyprus. It is made of clay and dated in the sixth century B.C. The antiquity of this toy is astonishing, even though we know that wheeled toys to be pushed, ridden, or pulled at the end of a string have always been popular. Now, 2,600 years later, you can make wheeled toys and still feel certain they will be well received.

All kinds of materials prove themselves suitable for wheeled toys in the hands of a craftsman. We have photographed examples of poured metal, sheet metal, wire, clay, fine hardwood, rough crate wood, plywood, pieces of trees, cardboard—even cloth. These toys vary from simple one-piece objects to the very complex, multi-piece toys.

Whatever toy you decide to put wheels on, the wheels are a problem to be solved separately. They must work well or the toy will be unsatisfactory. It may be helpful to examine commercially made toys to see how wheel and axle problems are solved, unless you take great pride in finding your own solutions. Wheel and axle assemblies in all-metal construction are not directly applicable to wood since the different qualities of the two materials require different handling. But one method of construction may suggest a variation that is workable.

All suggestions for wheels and axles in this chapter apply to wood because more people have access to wood and wood tools than to metal.

The toy to which you add wheels is usually a box shape or a solid block. About as simple a box as can be devised starts with a piece of wood at least ¾″ thick for the bottom. Next, cut the two ends which must be exactly the same width as the bottom piece and as high as you want the box to be deep. Nail and glue these two ends in place as shown in Drawing 24. Then measure along the base of these assembled three pieces to get the length of the sides. Fasten the sides in place with glue and nails along the bottom and up along the two end pieces. This completes a box which forms the basis of wagons, trains, and cages.

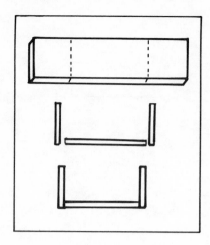

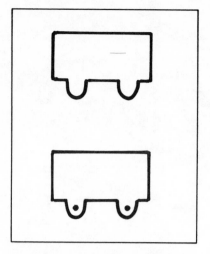

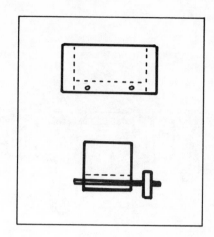

Drawing 24 Cut two ends and bottom of box from one piece of wood to assure perfect fit. Fasten ends to bottom as shown.

Drawing 25 After ends and bottom are assembled, saw sides with semi-circular tabs to fit. Drill holes for axles. Nail sides onto end/ bottom assembly.

Drawing 26 With sides nailed in place, drill axle hole through thick bottom.

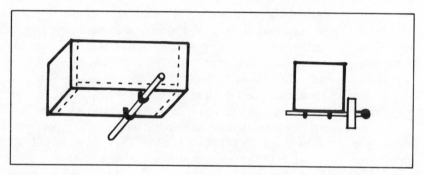

Drawing 27 Fasten axle and wheel assembly to toy bottom with U-shaped staples.

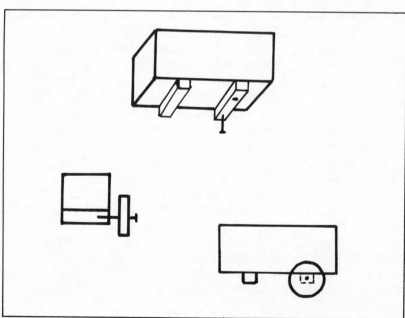

Drawing 28 Attach blocks to an existing box and nail wheels to the blocks.

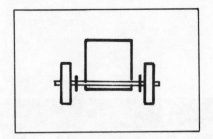

Drawing 29 *Small washers between wheel and side reduce friction.*

Here are some methods for adding wheels and axles:

1. The simplest wheels are the nonfunctional wheels, such as discs glued or nailed onto the side of a box. While these wheels do not turn, they may be essential to the appearance of the wagon or car. Wheels nailed to the legs of a table might make a non-rolling chariot. The covered wagon in Plate 177, designed to hold two children, was made with large plywood wheels nailed to 1" by 4" legs. Before these wheels were added, the structure looked like a box on legs.

2. Temporarily nail together the two boards from which the sides of the box are to be cut. Cut two tabs, one in front and one in the rear, big enough to allow a hole to be drilled for the axle, as shown in Drawing 25. On this toy, the wheels and the axle will be glued together and the axle will turn inside the tab holes.

3. When constructing the box, make the bottom of wood at least ¾" thick and drill the axle hole all the way through the bottom as in Drawing 26. To do this accurately, measure from each end and mark the drill spots on both sides of the toy. Drill from both sides—it's easier than trying to drill all the way through from one side. Again, insert the axle and glue the wheels to the axle. Avoid using plywood for this box bottom; plywood is made in layers and is not suitable for this kind of drilling.

4. If the box has a ¾"-thick bottom, the axle can be attached with U-shaped metal staples as shown in Drawing 27. The axle probably will not turn easily with this arrangement, so the wheels should be held on with a hub which allows them to turn freely on the axle.

5. After the block or constructed box is finished, fasten pieces of wood across the underside. Attach the wheels to the ends of these pieces with long nails so that the wheels turn on the nails. See Drawing 28.

All these examples of wheels and axles are fairly easy to assemble and have different advantages. Some are more quickly made than others, in case someone is standing at your elbow waiting for the toy. Some types of construction are much more durable than others. Which

176 *Charming little cars are blocks on wheels. 7" long, by Rob Denny.*

177 *Covered wagon made for
school play. Box is cardboard on 2″
by 2″ frame; wheels are large
plywood discs, nonturning. Sit
there headed West and wait. 5′
high, by Ruth Law.*

178 This 3″ long train engine is made of assorted woods, by Paul and Nancy Oltman.

179 Cars have faces on the front, with details done by a wood-burning tool. By Tom Freund.

180 Balsa wood racer. 4″ long, by Joel Aiken at age eight.

181 Duesenberg and touring car with riders, all-wood construction. By Shippen Swift.

182 Simple, charming hand-size cars made of ⅜″ hardwood. 3″ to 4″, by Eric Borgeson.

183 Small pine car by Joel Aiken cut on jigsaw. Note saw line showing entrance and exit of blade for cutting window.

184 Green Goo rides low on the road, but the bead wheels work surprisingly well. 3″ long, by Carolyn Bell.

185, 186 (Above) Discarded produce crates provided the wood for these wagons. 6″ and 9″, by Ruth Law.

187 (Below) Horse and covered wagon are early work of prolific five-year-old craftsman.

188 Mr. Toad's Cart, ready for the harness race. 3″, by Tom Laury.

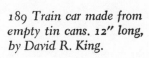
189 *Train car made from empty tin cans. 12″ long, by David R. King.*

one you use depends on what kind of a toy you have in mind. Do you want it to roll? Will a child ride on it? Do you want it immediately? Should it last a long while?

Don't overlook a variety of sources for wheels: Take the wheels and axles off worn-out toys, coaster wagons, or doll carriages; buy wheels from a craft shop; saw wheels out of wood; slice dowels of the right diameter; use beads, lids, or casters.

Plates 178 through 181 have wood-disc wheels with holes drilled through the toy bodies to accommodate the axle. Wheels are glued to the axles. Axles must be approximately ¼″ longer than the combined thickness of the body and two wheels. In order to prevent the wheel from rubbing against the body, it is a good idea to slip a thin metal washer on the axle between wheel and body, as in Drawing 29.

The train shown in Plate 178 is assembled from several kinds of wood. Details are added to cars in Plate 179 with a wood-burning tool. Handsomely made of hardwood, the chunky durable constructions in Plate 182 might just outlast the Detroit products. The little car shown in Plate 183 has bumps sawed at the base to represent wheels, though they are nonfunctional. Green Goo is delivered in a small wood block car (Plate 184) with ½″ beads nailed on for wheels.

The basic box toys of Plates 185 and 186 are made from produce crates found in grocery store trash bins. These toys duplicate the construction of most produce crates in that they have thin sides attached to thick ends. In addition, the wheels are made from ¾″ crate wood that was cut into 3″ squares, sanded clean, and silk-screened with the spoked wheel pattern. Silk screening is a multicopy process and lends itself very well to the four-at-a-time requirements of toy wheels. After printing, these wheels are sawed out and drilled exactly at the center with a hole to fit the dowel axle. (Drill bits and dowels come in the same series of sizes.) Drilling the hole ever so slightly off center gives the assembled toy an amusing, carefree wobble.

The toad wagon in Plate 188 is in a category by itself for short-lived toys. A young boy spent about eight minutes making the two-wheeled cart, while the toad hunkered down beside him, waiting. Toad spent about two minutes in harness before he went on about his other toad business.

The unusual train in Plate 189 is the work of a small boy. It is basically a pair of empty food cans connected with black friction tape. These are nailed to a flat board with axles attached, as shown in Drawing 28. The wheels are nailed onto the axle boards. The whole effect is crude and boylike and was not abandoned until the boy was a twenty-five-year-old man.

Trains made to resemble the iron horses of America's adventurous past are very popular toys. Color Plate 40 shows a pull-toy train made of assembled blocks. The engine, a box car, and a wobbly caboose connect to one another with hooks and eye screws. The wood is undercoated and painted with high-gloss enamel. Wheels are slices of birch dowels.

Two additional trains are shown in color. Color Plate 39 shows an imaginative clay sculpture of a train that hauls or runs on cherry-topped ice cream cones. The result is very festive. Christmas seals are shown in Color Plate 42. The little stamps are glued to thin pine and sawed out.

An entirely different approach to train making is shown in Plates 190 and 191. The natural state of the logs gives the train a timeless, classic appeal. It is as durable as it looks and would be especially inviting for the child who gets hassled for chipping the paint on a new toy. The weathering cracks which go almost to the center of each wheel detract nothing from this rugged toy. The train designer managed to drill two holes through the body of the log so uniformly that all four wheels touch down at once.

A funny train results from the unlikely combination of subject matter and working materials in Plate 194. The train cars are made of cleverly combined fabrics stuffed with batting. Cars are attached to each other with tabs and snaps. The wheels are made separately and attached with upholsterers' buttons. A sewn and stuffed locomotive is reminiscent of Claes Oldenburg's soft sculptures of hard-edge objects.

190 *Crewman with wood train.*

108

191 Massive, primitive-looking toy
is made of sections of natural log.
15" long, by Craig Thorburn.

192 Cart made from clay rolled out
with a rolling pin has stick axles.
4" long, by Ruth Law.

193 Brightly painted wood circus
wagon ready for loading. 7" high,
by Ruth Law.

194 Soft train—an incongruous
mix of material and subject
by Lenore Schwartz Goodell. 66"
long.

The two plywood sides of the brightly painted circus cage in Plate 193 were temporarily nailed together for sawing. When the completed shape had been cut, the sides were pulled apart and nailed to the roof and floor of the cage. This assured identical designs for the two sides. A hole drilled through the cage bottom at front and rear holds the axles, to which wheels are permanently glued. The wheels were sliced from 2″ birch dowels.

The crude clay toy in Plate 192 was made by rolling out the clay, cutting the pieces, and fitting them together. Four axle tabs are attached to the underside of the box. All holes for axles are made before the clay is fired. Wheels are epoxy-glued to the whittled stick axles. The fanciful vehicles in Plates 196 and 197 are the work of a ceramist. He seems intent on combining all the glories of Primitive Car and Supercar. He works in stoneware and employs glazes to make his elaborate details even more realistic.

The remarkable weight lifter on wheels in Plate 195 is made of cast pewter. As he deftly holds the barbells high over his head, he is balancing himself on the axle between two giddily tilted wheels. Florence Pettit made all the pieces of this toy by pouring melted pewter into molds carved from sand-core.

When J. R. Peirano set out on an assignment to make an exceptional

195 *Cast pewter weight lifter holds perch on axle and raises weights over his head without popping a button. 7″ high, by Florence Pettit.*

196 *The Eddcell is a flivver hard pressed to keep up with its mighty engine. It is 18″, of glazed stoneware, by Edd Burke.*

197 *Jeep Dream tilts back in imitation of high acceleration even while motionless. 13″ long, by Edd Burke.*

198 (Above) Sculptured wood tricycle, 39" high, by J. R. Peirano.

199 (Above right) Handsome wire sculpture is an old-fashioned tricycle. Wheels do not turn, but who cares? 7" high, by Rick Columbini.

200 This snail's pace is not like most. He is made of firmly stuffed patchwork and sits on a board with casters. 20" high, by Lilo Nassé.

toy, he succeeded with his all-wood tricycle, shown in Plate 198. It is sculptured from an assortment of exotic woods and can be ridden.

Pieces of small-diameter wire were welded together to make the realistic old-fashioned tricycle in Plate 199. The wheels do not turn, but no matter.

For a child to know a toymaker who can fulfill his needs is a great thing, but Bogi Nassé knows a toymaker who can exceed his needs. His mother, Lilo Nassé, created a snail (Plate 200) on wheels before anyone could know it was needed. Her snail has stuffed purple feelers, which double as reins, and a shy smile. It is made of a long, pieced crazy-quilt tube that is firmly stuffed and coiled. The snail is attached to a wood base with highly maneuverable casters set on the underside. The snail is about 20″ high and likes to give rides.

In other more self-sufficient times, toymaking was something older people did for the children. It was a natural and vital part of the interaction of the family unit. This activity on the part of adults implied an intrinsic worth in toys. From a child's point of view, Doug Parmeter and Rob Denny must be regarded as ideal fathers: Making toys involves most of their time. Their exceptionally well-made toys have

201 *Skillful workmanship and attention to detail result in the all-wood biplane which just might be airworthy. 24″ wingspan, by Doug Parmeter.*

202 *Pickup truck from the good old days is made of willow, assembled with brass nails. 18″ long, bumper to bumper. By Doug Parmeter.*

112

24. *Apple Doll, 14",*
    by Alice Peterson

25. *Jack-in-the-box (out of his*
    box), 2', by Jude Crossland

26. *Mouse Couple, 4",*
    by Pippa Sher and Babs Kavanaugh

27. *Jester, 5",*
    by Babs Kavanaugh

28. *Grandpa Mouse, 4",*
    by Babs Kavanaugh

29. *Stocking Face Puppet, 14″,*
by Jean Ray Laury

30. *Jumping Jack,*
by Terrie Sullivan Floyd

31. *Marionette,*
by Terrie Sullivan Floyd

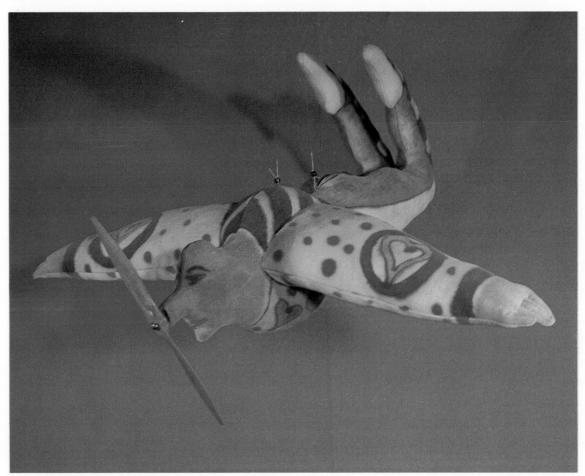

32. *Airplane Man, 17″ from propeller to knees (20″ wingspan), by Lenore Davis*

33. *Fred and Mildred Go to the Prom, 40″ by 42″, by Susan Morrison*

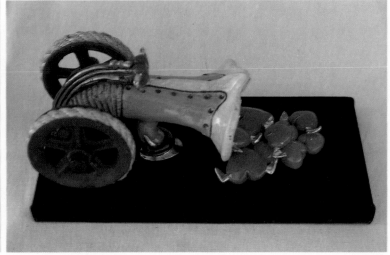

34. *Heart Cannon, 18″, by Bill Burke*

35. *Seymour and Sylvester, 40″,*
by Poppy Kwong

36. *Barn, 12″, by Tom Freund*

37. *Finger Puppet, 4",*
    by Tamelin McNutt, age 10

38. *Red Riding Hood, 3",*
    by Jean Ray Laury

39. *Ceramic Train, by Bill Burke*

40. *Wood Train, 20″ long,
   by Ruth Law*

41. *Nest, 4′ diameter,
   by Elsbeth Ramos*

42. *TB Christmas Seal Train, 4″
   long, by Ruth Law*

43. *Macaroni Wagons, 2″ long,*
    by Ruth Law

44. *Circle Swing, 9″ across,*
    by Ruth Law

45. *Postage Stamp Block, 1″*
    square, by Ruth Law

46. *Ceramic Block, 4″ to 13″*
    square, by Edd Burke

47. *Blocks, 2″ square,*
    by Jean Ray Laury

48. *Batik Angel, 16″ tall,*
    by Margaret "Mog" Miller

49. *Batik Beast, 24″ long,*
    by Kay Schneider

50. *Welded Car, 5″ high,*
    by Rick Columbini

203 Milk truck has steel rod axles and curtain rings for tires. Compartment full of blocks offers play business for a small child. 18" long, by Doug Parmeter.

204 Versatile ride-on truck made of plywood. Note simple dowel construction. 20" long, by Rob Denny.

205 Pilot and stewardess on airplane, by Doug Parmeter.

206 Shaped plywood critter-carriage by Rob Denny.

great appeal for children. There is just enough realistic detail to intrigue any literal-minded child and enough versatility to appeal to everyone else. Doug's biplane and pickup truck in Plates 201 and 202 are made from many pieces of carefully cut and fitted hardwood. Only the tires, made of wood curtain rings, and the steel axles, held by acorn nuts, are of commercial manufacture. His larger ride-on toys, such as the airplane in Plates 205 and 208, show equal care and attention to design and finishing detail. Rob Denny makes extensive use of plywood in building his toys. They are simple and well-designed, intended to withstand the hard use of engineers, ferry captains, and crane operators with a no-nonsense approach to their play. His toys appear in Plates 204, 206, 207, and 209.

Some toymakers hug their creativity close to them. Some enjoy the sharing, underscoring their sense of community with others rather than their individuality. Any human being might impulsively embrace a stranger in a moment of shared feeling. The same spontaneity and warmth might prompt someone to conceive of the breath-taking Heart Cannon shown in Plate 210. The cannon, a weapon of large-scale destruction, is loaded with winged hearts and aimed at random. Armament experts, add "overlove" to your vocabulary and consider your strategic noses tweaked by Bill Burke!

207 Large ride-on toy train engine, with coal car following. Plywood construction. 20" long, by Rob Denny.

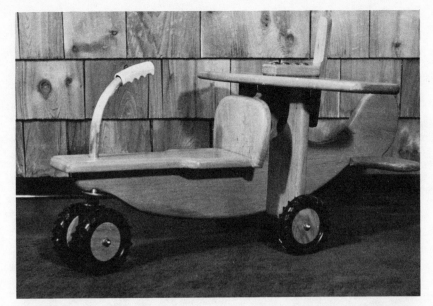

208 Large ride-on airplane was made with great care and skill from alderwood. Rubber tired wheels are of commercial manufacture. 34″ long, by Doug Parmeter.

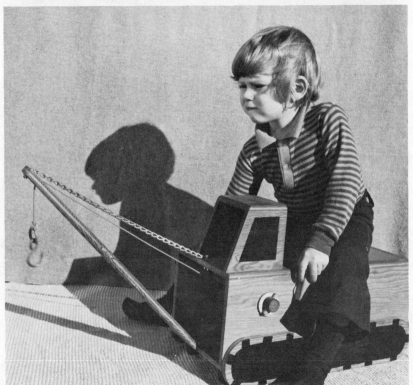

209 Sturdy crane with moving parts keeps young workman very busy. 20″ cab, by Rob Denny.

210 Heart Cannon of glazed stoneware clay, slab construction. By Bill Burke.

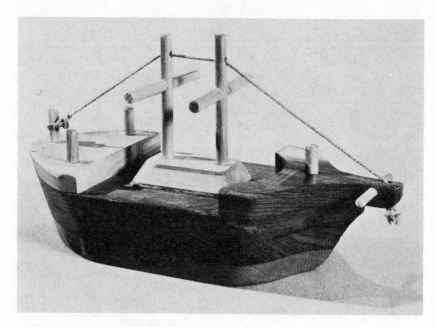

211 *Laminated boards and ½″ doweling are the basic materials of this pond-worthy craft. 13″ long, by Richard Graybill.*

212 *Drifting soundlessly, a simple sturdy boat captivates a child's imagination for endless hours.*

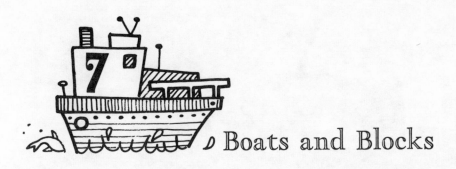

Boats and Blocks

When "The owl and the pussycat went to sea
in a beautiful pea green boat,"

they set out on an adventure that still intrigues children. Ships at sea
always sail to far-off exotic ports. Even rub-a-dub-dub's three men in a
tub had grand visions of where they hoped to sail. The lure of the sea
has not faded, even in the jet age. Boats are still among the best of the
old favorite toys. If a pond or stream is available, the time consumed in
nautical adventures is never ending. To admirals and pirates, even a
puddle, bath tub, or wading pool offers a good place to launch a simple craft. For a child, the boat need be nothing more than a scrap of
wood with a string attached. For a toymaker with a few tools, there
are infinite possibilities.

The boat in Plate 211 is made from a series of laminated boards.
Holes are drilled topside so that ½" dowels can be set into place and
glued. The finished boat has several coats of waterproof finish. Toymaker Richard Graybill keeps a fleet of these boats anchored in a tub
of water.

The magnificent ark in Plates 213 and 214 is filled with Noah's animals. It is not made to be used in the water, and still has the wheels
which made it maneuverable before the forty days and forty nights of
rain began. Tom Freund, an inventive and meticulous toymaker, fashioned the ark from cottonwood and walnut. For him toys are alive—a
good toy "puts you into a fantasy world where the toy lives and breathes
and works." The ark can be disassembled to reveal the interior. A ramp
leads from ground level up to the hatch. The animals are sawed and
carved, then painted in pastel colors with acrylics. Another of Tom's
toys is shown in Color Plate 36.

Children love making their own boats and will devise simple ones
of scrap materials. See Drawing 30. Waxed containers make a good waterproof base, and when two are lashed together, they make a very stable boat. Milk cartons, cut in half, are shown in Drawing 31. If there is
any water around, children will figure out a way to make a boat. See
Plate 215.

213, 214 *Noah's ark, 22" long, is constructed of cottonwood and walnut.
The hatch opens when the peg on deck is lifted. Straggling in to board
the ark are bright acrylic-colored animals, sawed and carved.
By Tom Freund.*

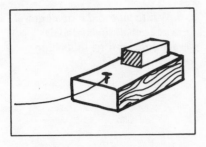

Drawing 30 Scrap blocks of wood are all a child needs to make a boat. Add a nail and string to make retrieval simple.

215 Give any child some seaweed, a piece of driftwood, and about thirty seconds, and he'll give you a boat.

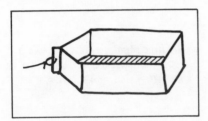

Drawing 31 Milk cartons, cut in half, make boats that can be launched in sixty seconds. Add a box inside to make a tug, or staple a mast to the end to convert it into a sailboat.

216 Who can resist setting a boat to sail at the water's edge?

217 A Viking boat from wood scraps by seven-year-old Cass McNutt.

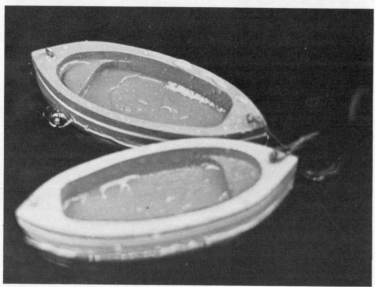

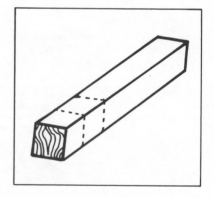

218 *White pine and a small dowel or pencil are all the materials needed for this little sailboat, 9" long. By Ruth Law.*

219 *Three separate pieces of wood are cut, then stacked and glued to make little fishermen's dories.*

Drawing 32 Pine 2"×2" can be cut in 2" lengths to form blocks.

A seven-year-old boy made the Viking ship in Plate 217 from scrap-wood pieces. The sail is paper, the base plywood, so water will eventually soak and warp it. However, it'll dry out and the sail is easily replaced. Plates 218 and 219 show some easily made boats that require only a little time at the saw with some wood scraps.

Blocks, like boats, are traditional and old favorite playthings. They are among the simplest of all toys, yet offer so many possibilities for various kinds of play that they remain a favorite beyond the childhood years. Observe how many parents are unable to leave their kids' blocks alone.

Simple wood blocks (cubes) may be cut from pine. See Drawing 32.

220 *Felt appliqué on 4″ squares form the sides of this block. The cube is stuffed with polyester batting and slip-stitched shut. By Jean Ray Laury.*

221 *Embroidered fabrics sewn together to make blocks were reinforced with boxes on the inside. 12″ high, by Jorjanna Lundgren.*

222 *Squares crocheted of bright-colored yarn are embroidered with the letters of a child's name. 5″ cube, by Mark Law.*

Woods are available in standard 2″ by 2″ or 4″ by 4″ boards. If you want accurate cubes, measure the width of the board and then cut lengths of that same measurement. Remember that some wood will be lost from the thickness of the saw blade. Many lumberyards will do this cutting for you; some will charge a cutting fee. Random-sized blocks are easiest to cut and offer greater variations in block constructions.

The blocks in Plate 223 are cut from a 2″ by 2″ board. They are then sanded, lightly stained, and left to dry. The designs shown were silk-screen printed onto card-weight paper, then glued to the wood. Pictures from greeting cards may also be used to decorate wood blocks. Avoid pictures with printing on the back as this sometimes comes through when glued. See Color Plate 48 for blocks decorated with letters, numbers, and pictures cut from magazines and books. Children's old damaged books provide illustrations on heavy paper, and some are just right for blocks. Color Plate 45 pictures another unusual block—the sides are covered with colorful German Christmas stamps showing detailed engravings of traditional toys.

Laminated woods take advantage of grain patterns and offer handsome decorative features to the building blocks in Plate 224. After the pieces were laminated and cut into blocks, a stain was used to accent the linear patterns.

Toymakers and sculptors are often playful in their approach to materials and ideas. They may "toy" with an idea so that satire, humor, and social commentary emerge together in a plaything that also incorporates their interests in the visual and tactile aspects of the toy. Some of these toys are designed for adults. It is the toymaker who plays; we share his amusement and are entertained by his wit and skill. Most of us love having these toys around us, whether we handle them or not.

One such toy, in Color Plate 46 is a stack of blocks by Edd Burke. They're obviously not children's building blocks, but they are toylike. There is a delightful surprise element found in toys that challenge a preconceived idea. Certainly a nostalgic association with children's blocks evokes a response, and the unlikely choice of material commands a second look. Whether it's categorized as a funky sculpture or a sophisticated toy matters less than the humor and intrigue of its form.

Fabric blocks are great for very young children just learning to pick things up and move them about. They are also great for the toymaker who enjoys needlework, since the variations are unlimited. Whatever way you like to work, the results can probably be used on a block! These include needlepoint, knitting, crochet, weaving, appliqué, batik, patchwork, and embroidery. Plates 220, 221, 222, and 225 show appliqué, embroidery, and crochet used on blocks. Almost any scrap materials can be utilized in these.

Blocks that fit together were designed by Arthur Lind in Plate 226. Because the arms of both figure shapes are of the same length (half the body width) they fit together in a surprising number of ways. As a craftsman who makes toys all day every day, Arthur Lind is quite sensi-

223 Chunks of 2″ by 2″ pine make good blocks. Silk-screened designs are glued on, then a clear finishing coat is added. By Jean Ray Laury.

224 Lamination accents the beautiful wood-grain patterns in these blocks by James Fuller. 7″ to 8″ tall.

tive to the tactile and visual qualities of toys. These are as important to play as the mechanics or mathematics of the ways toys function. These figures appeal to both children and adults. Arthur feels that "There really isn't much of an age factor in toys. I find that children like to play with the same toys I like to play with—they like the things adults like."

226 *Pyramid People fit together and stack in a variety of ways. Cut from laminated woods, the figures are 6" high and 1" thick. By Arthur Lind.*

225 *Yarn-embroidered patchwork squares cover foam-rubber blocks that stack to make a doll. 5", by Jorjanna Lundgren.*

123

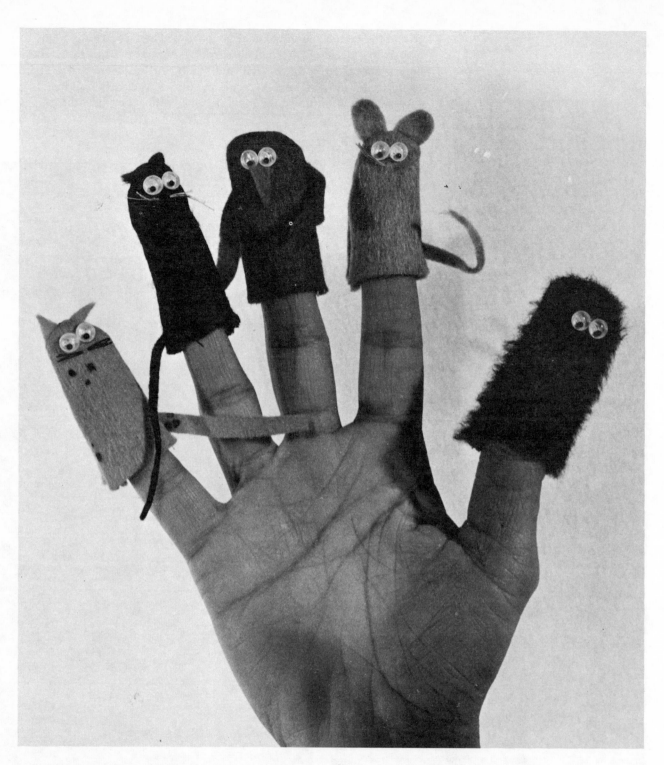

227 Arch-shaped finger puppets
form a sharp-eyed group at arm's
length. The goo-goo eyes are
available at hobby shops. 2″ tall,
by Pippa Sher.

8 Puppets

An animated, automated figure or doll that cries, moves, walks, and talks leaves little to the imagination. The child becomes a mere spectator. If the child animates the figure, however, he puts life into it . . . it becomes an extension of the child's ideas. The youngster who only observes may be entertained or amused, but it is a limited involvement since his own ideas and thoughts are not expressed.

Puppets and marionettes offer a classic opportunity for involvement between child and toy. The extent to which the manipulator absorbs the identity of the puppet (or vice versa) is varied. The possibility for strong identification is evidenced in the use of puppetry by speech therapists, psychologists, teachers, and, more spectacularly, in films such as *Lili*. If you ever have observed children at a puppet show, you have seen their total absorption in the seemingly "real" puppets. If you have helped children make and operate puppets, you have seen the ecstatic excitement as they *become* these believable characters. It is revealing to listen to children playing various roles with their puppets —your role for instance.

Puppets are simple doll or animal shapes that fit over the hand or a finger. Since they are hollow, without bodies, something is needed to hold them erect and animate them. Usually the hand and sometimes a stick is used for this purpose. All puppets are held and manipulated from below. A table top makes a good stage setting, as children can reach up to the table edge with a hand puppet, while kneeling or squatting behind the table.

A marionette is a similar figure needing animation, but it is manipulated from above. Strings attached to head and limbs allow the operator to give a remarkable variety of positions to the figures. The marionette requires much more practice and skill to control than a puppet.

Between these two basic methods of animation (from below by hand or finger, or from above by strings) there are endless variations. You or your children may devise more. String puppets, jumping jacks, stick puppets, shadow puppets, and marionettes are all variations that are described or illustrated in this chapter.

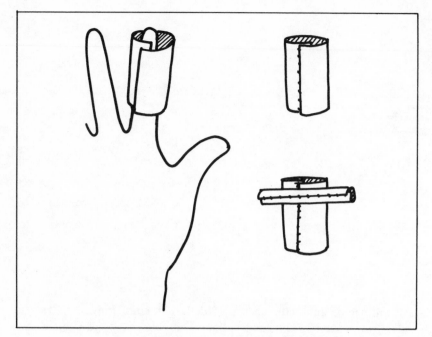

Drawing 33 A rectangle of felt can be wrapped sleevelike around a finger, then slip-stitched in place. A small rolled tube of felt is added to make the arms.

Drawing 34 Two keyhole shapes are stitched together and stuffed to make a head, then inserted into the body shape and stitched in place. Features, hair, hands, and clothes may be added in a variety of ways.

Among the simplest of all puppets to make are the finger puppets shown in Drawings 33 and 34. In a matter of minutes a few scraps can be transformed into a new personality. Wrapped around a finger, a rectangle of felt forms the easiest basic structure to which a head and arms may be attached. The puppets pictured in Color Plates 37 and 38 are made in this way.

An even simpler method uses two arch-shaped forms, putting head and body together. Arms can be inserted between the two body parts.

*Drawing 35 Two arch shapes are
cut so that when stitched together
a finger easily fits inside. Hair,
arms, or ears can be inserted into
that seam.*

*Drawing 36 By cutting the head,
arms, and body parts all in one
piece, the assembly is simplified.*

Another way to form puppets is to cut arms, head, and body all in one
piece. See Drawings 35 and 36. Two identical shapes are cut and
joined. Wild beasts, sewn from fake fur, form the finger puppets in
Plate 228. An arch-shaped Red Riding Hood is shown in Plate 229.
Felts are used for the handful of birds and creatures in Plate 227.

The pig and horse in Plate 230 use two profile shapes sewn together.
This is an especially good way for animal puppets to be constructed where
the profile is essential in depicting the animal. This method is illustrated by the animals in Drawing 37, as well as by the man in Plate
231. Other finger puppets are shown in Color Plates 26 and 27.

Simple stick puppets by a six-year-old are shown in Plate 232. Wood
forks suggested the basic body forms for a cat and a queen. These are
kept upright and moved by holding them at the bottom edge of the
stick. The same method works well on a puppet stage. Larger puppets

127

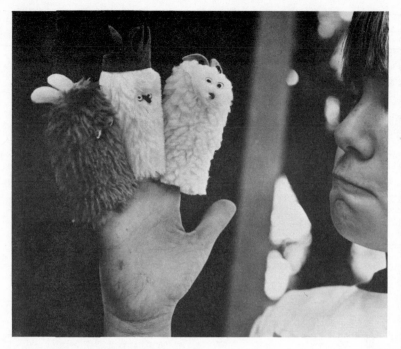

228 *Shaggy and gruff finger puppets evoke a scowl from the boy who holds them. Each is made from arch-shaped pieces of fake fur. 2″ tall, by Jackie Vermeer.*

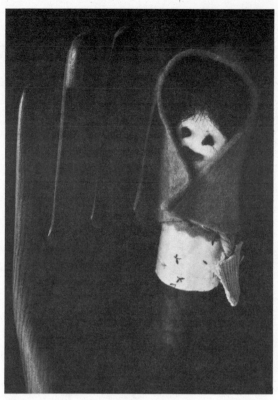

229 *Little Red Riding Hood warms a finger with her felt hood and yarn hair. 3″ tall.*

230 *Two profile forms of felt were sewn together for this dancing pig and prancing steed—3″ tall. Pig by Pippa Sher.*

231 *A finger prince with yarn hair retains his dignity while waiting to be slipped over a finger. The face is machine stitched, then turned so that the seam is on the inside. From the Dickens Faire.*

make use of a wood dowel or ruler or a section of yardstick to hold the puppet head erect. See Drawing 38.

A hand puppet should be made to fit the hand of the person who wears it. Usually the index finger holds the head up, though sometimes two fingers are used. See Drawing 40.

A cotton sock provides a hand puppet with head and body. The giraffe in Plate 233 has bead and felt features.

Bets Barnard's delightful hand puppets in Plates 234 and 235 are made with appliquéd faces. The heads are sewn, then slipped over a cardboard tube which is padded with batting. Yarns are loop-stitched over and over for marvelously full hairdos. In this kind of puppet the

Drawing 37 Various animals in this drawing were copied from finger puppets by Pippa Sher and Babs Kavanaugh.

Drawing 38 Paint-mixing sticks, with tongue depressors added for arms, make good stick puppets.

232 To a child, even a wooden fork has possibilities. The stick puppet cat and a queen are drawn with marking pen and dressed in pipe cleaners. By Liz Laury, at age five.

Drawing 39 A rubber or Styrofoam ball can be pushed onto the end of a stick (bamboo, dowel, or pencil), a cross-stick added, and the simple stick puppet is ready.

Drawing 40 Hand puppets can be made so that the head fits over one or two fingers.

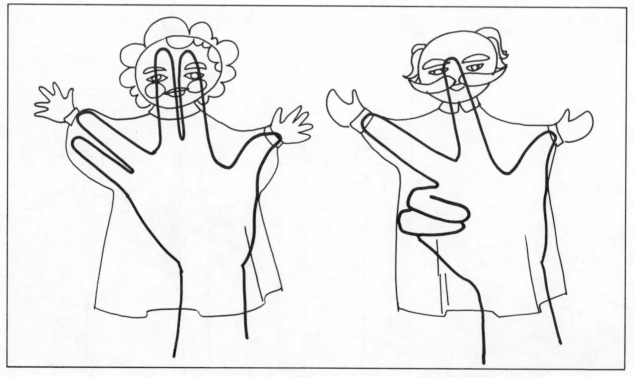

entire hand goes inside with the thumb controlling one arm, the two end fingers controlling the second arm, leaving two for the head.

Susan Morrison's puppets are among the most imaginative of all. Basically, they are simple felt forms, with mouths set into the front of the puppets' face. An energetic use of small details gives the puppets a complexity that belies the simplicity of their construction. See Plates 236 through 240.

An amusing dragon's head puppet is shown in Plate 241. It is not a true puppet, but a head that can be operated by hand. A milk carton, cut in half, is covered in felt and then eyes, teeth, and other features

233 *A giraffe stretches his neck from wrist to elbow in a hand puppet made from a sock. The toe is slit open and fabric inserted to suggest the inside of a mouth. 10½" long, by Babs Kavanaugh.*

234 *The swashbuckling one-eyed pirate seems less than ominous as he waits for someone to put him into action. Two cut pieces of fabric form the simple construction over a padded cardboard tube. 9", by Bets Barnard.*

235 *Hand puppet with felt appliqué features. 9", by Bets Barnard.*

are added. The uncut bottom side of the milk box forms a hinge which lets the jaw swing open.

Stuffed nylon stockings make excellent puppet forms. Stitches taken on the surface pull the features into prominence, and the lower end of the soft stocking provides a good tunnel for the hand. Once the head is formed, a garment with arms attached is added as for any other hand puppet. To help hold the head upright, leave a tunnel in the stocking head so that a finger can be inserted. See Drawing 41. Or use a small cardboard tube (from tissue paper or paper toweling) to which padding and stockings are added. See Plates 242 and 243, and Color Plate 29.

Animated figures, like those shown in Plates 244 through 246, are fairly simple to do. Elizabeth Fuller has batik-painted her figures first, then applied the fabric to cardboard. The cut cardboard shapes are then joined with brass paper-fasteners (the kind with which all school children are familiar—they have a rounded head and two flat prongs that spread open).

The figures can be cut entirely from cardboard and decorated with marking pens or paints. One possibility is shown in Drawing 42. A

236 A cow chews peacefully on a bunch of daisies as the hand moves the nose back and forth. 12″ high, by Susan Morrison.

237 Detail showing the awesome interior of the cow's mouth, fully opened.

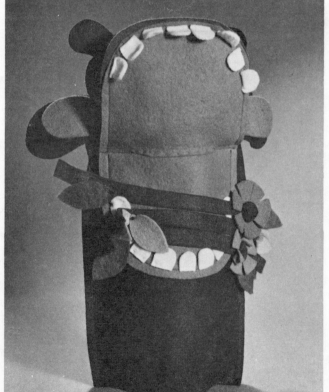

Drawing 41 Dacron batting is wrapped around a cardboard tube and secured at the bottom with masking tape. A nylon stocking is pulled over all, tied in place, and then it's ready for stitching in facial features.

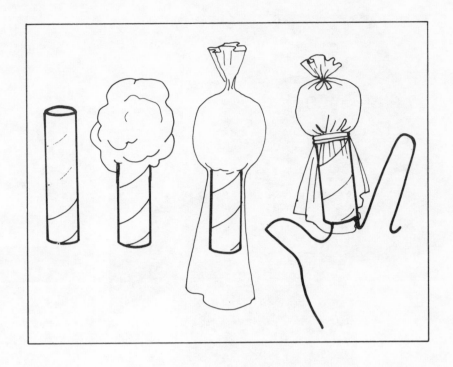

238 Pig puppet makes room for the entire hand so that the fingers, with thumb opposed, can open the mouth. 13", by Susan Morrison.

239 Detail of the pig showing his oink coming out.

133

240 Bird hand puppet (probably a stool pigeon revealing secrets). By Susan Morrison.

241 A hand-operated dragon snaps his powerful jaws shut from the hinged end. He is made over a milk carton, 6″ long. By Alison Law.

242 Stuffed nylon-stocking puppet. 14″ tall, by Jean Ray Laury.

243 Girlie on the right says the girlie on the left is a nylon-stocking puppet made over a small cardboard tube. 10″, by Jean Ray Laury.

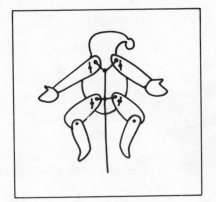

Drawing 43 *Jumping jacks do knee jerks and dances when you pull the connecting strings. The jacks can be tied in various ways as shown.*

Drawing 42 *An animated stick puppet has arms and legs attached with brass brads. This lets them move into different positions.*

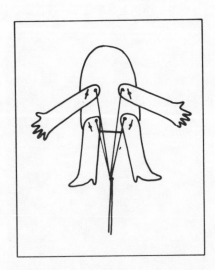

Drawing 44 *Add a string or a hole at the top by which the animal may be hung.*

Drawing 45 *Simple jumping-jack string harness.*

244 *Musician, a 9" animated figure, is made in pieces which are then joined with brass clasps. By Elizabeth Fuller.*

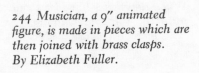

245 (Left) Rooster, batik fabric on cardboard. By Elizabeth Fuller.

246 (Right) The Tattooed Man gets his elaborate markings through batik painting combined with printing. Parts of the man are then joined so that the arms and legs can be set into a variety of positions. 24″ tall, by Elizabeth Fuller.

247 Marionette of the Big Bad Wolf shows strings running from the beast to a stick at the top. When the stick is tilted back and forth, the wolf appears to run. By Cam Smith, at age twelve.

136

common form of this with which everyone is familiar is the cardboard skeleton children delight in playing with at Halloween. The jointed leg bones allow the skeleton to assume playful, dancelike positions. If the brass fasteners are closed loosely, the figure will dance when moved rapidly.

These figures can be animated further by attaching strings to make the traditional Jumping Jack. Drawings 43 and 45 show two ways by which strings may be attached. The jack can be hung from a single string, as in Drawing 44, or held at the top. The string is then pulled at the bottom, causing erratic jumping, flailing, or kicking. See Color Plate 30 for a more elaborate jack made from wood.

Marionettes are more difficult to make as well as to operate. Many good references are available for those who wish to pursue this exacting and intriguing art. Color Plate 31 shows an example of an elaborate hand-carved figure. A simpler one, made by a junior high student, is shown in Plate 247.

Puppets are easy-to-make, inexpensive toys that can be totally absorbing for dramatists of all ages. Don't overlook the possibilities of even the simplest of these—the brown paper-bag puppet in Plate 248.

248 (Left) Nervous hands belie sleepy casual expression on the shopping bag.

Drawing 46 The arch-shaped finger puppet forms a basis for any of these simple figures.

249 Pancake rabbit, 8″, waits for
butter and jam.

250 Race through breakfast on a
pancake roadster. Small spoonfuls
of dough make the wheels. These
tiny pancakes are turned, then the
car body is poured over the wheels.

251 Wild Syrup Guzzlers stalk
the breakfast table.

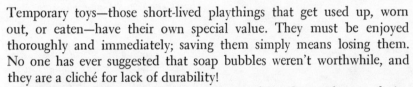

Temporary Toys

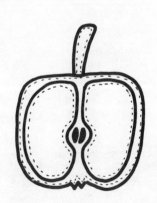

Temporary toys—those short-lived playthings that get used up, worn out, or eaten—have their own special value. They must be enjoyed thoroughly and immediately; saving them simply means losing them. No one has ever suggested that soap bubbles weren't worthwhile, and they are a cliché for lack of durability!

Edible materials provide a great range for ephemeral toys; fruits, vegetables, baked things such as cookies, gingerbread, bread dough, baker's clay, pancakes, or even less permanent foods such as ice cream and gelatins.

Flapjack animals march across breakfast tables daily, traveling from griddle to plate to mouth (Plates 249–251). Consuming the animal object is certainly part of the joy. If you've been the creator of a pancake horse, you may have heard a hungry youngster comment as he eats. It does not seem to be regarded as any act of violence—rather, it is a way of letting the horse become a part of the child: "I feel the horse in my tummy . . . it's getting out to my toes . . . see, I can gallop." The horse becomes a part of the child's body, so that the child becomes what he consumes. Eating the animal becomes a magical process.

Cookie-cutter sandwiches, in Plate 258, offer another acceptable means of consuming the object of one's affections. Since the first gingerbread boy sprang to life from the Old Woman's oven, gingerbread people have been a favorite of children. Some are left in the rich brown color of the cookie, which results from the molasses and spices used in baking. Other cutouts, made without molasses and with white sugar, come out of the oven a light brown or pale yellow. A few raisins provide the features. They may be more elaborately decorated with frostings and cake-decorating tubes.

Breads and cookies in the forms of people and animals are known throughout the world. Among the most common are the brilliantly painted animals and figures from Ecuador, the human figures of dough and sugar from Mexico, the Portuguese alligator-shaped breads, the Dutch windmill and toy cookies, and decorative cookies from Germany and the Scandinavian countries. There are few countries in the world where some effort has not been made to add a decorative and

252 Gingerbread figures, made with a store-bought cookie cutter.

253 Cookie horse was frosted and decorated with much affection and finger licking by a child.

254, 255 Animal crackers, painted with acrylic paints, make wild beasts worthy of the deepest jungle.

256, 257, 258 The common cookie cutter can unleash a herd of animals in any kitchen. Peanut butter cements slices together so that they stand more easily.

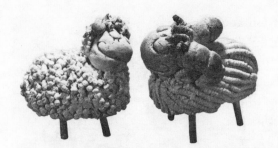

259 Bread-dough ram and ewe.
*Before baking, dowel legs are
inserted in the dough to make
holes. They are removed for baking,
then glued in place later. 4" high,
by Joan Weldon.*

260 A flock of lambs smile from
*their pen. All are made from a
bread-dough mix by Joan Weldon.
Pen is 10" square.*

261 The sun bather, a painted
*bread figure, has jointed arms and
legs. By Lilo Nassé.*

262 A fabulous contraption flies
*out of Lilo Nassé's kitchen,
powered by a bread propeller.*

263 (Left) Bread-dough engine,
*7" high, was baked in parts and
then assembled. By Lilo Nassé.*

playful quality to certain foods. Gelatin molds in the shape of fish are common, as are wedding cakes with edible sugar brides and grooms perched precariously atop.

Another ephemeral toy, though not an edible one, is the painted animal cracker. Using acrylic paints, cookie-artist Liz Laury painted the animal crackers (or animal cookies) available at grocery stores. See Plates 254 and 255. A final coating of a plastic varnish helps discourage ants. Watercolor paints will work, but food coloring will leave the cookies edible.

A good way of adding edible color to any cookies (gingerbread, sugar cookies, or even the already baked animal cookies) is to mix food color with egg yolk. One yolk is enough to decorate several dozen cookies. Use part of one yolk to mix with a color, add a few drops of water as needed. Apply to the cookie shapes that have been cut out with cookie cutters and placed on a baking sheet. Bake as usual. The egg yolk gives a shiny glaze and the colors stay brilliant. Ready-baked cookies can be painted, then placed on a cookie sheet and slipped into a hot oven briefly. Just a few minutes will set the egg and color.

Both gingerbread and sugar-cookie dough tend to rise in baking, which distorts the design of the cookie pattern. To reduce this problem, add an extra ½ cup of flour and knead the dough to make it less short and more "tired."

Somewhat more permanent than cookies are the very popular bread dough or baker's clay toys. Joan Weldon's sheep in Plates 259 and 260 got their curly wool when she pressed the dough through a garlic press. She made the sheep by first forming heads and bodies. She then pressed the end of a small wood dowel into the body to make an indentation for the legs. After baking, cut sections of the dowels were worked into the holes and glued in place to make legs. Fence posts were done similarly. Joan used a mixture of:

4 c. flour
1 c. salt
1½ c. water.

The dough is kneaded thoroughly for about 5 or 10 minutes. Then it is rolled, pressed, pinched, squeezed, and shaped. A fairly tough dough works best, so work or knead in more flour if needed.

Use a little water to make joining parts adhere. When the dough toys are prepared, they may be placed on a cookie sheet and baked at 350 degrees for about an hour. The time will depend upon the thickness of the dough pieces being baked.

Lilo Nassé's marvelous bread-dough creations are shown in Plates 261 through 263. Propellers, wheels, arms, and legs are all made as separate pieces and assembled after baking. Features, bikinis, pilot's helmets, and details are added with a small brush and paint.

There are numerous variations of the recipes available for gingerbread cookies, sugar cookies, and bread dough or baker's clay. Which one you use depends upon your particular need for detail, permanence, or edibility.

The ephemeral nature of all these toys is part of their value and charm. They must be enjoyed now, for they may soon be gone. We

264 *A tiny waif takes shape from discarded bubble gum! While not a recommended medium, any creative child will form animals and figures from whatever is available. By Alison Law at age ten.*

265 *Camellia buds and blossoms, held together with pieces of toothpicks, form full-skirted ladies.*

encourage this when we give children chocolate rabbits, sugar babies, and pecan turtles. We expect that they'll be bitten, chewed, and swallowed. Maple-sugar candies in the form of girls and boys, Indian chiefs in headdresses, or animals are meant to be decapitated and devoured.

Another kind of ephemeral toy is made from flowers. The toy may last only twenty or thirty minutes in warm weather. Hollyhocks are one of the most common flowers for dolls. Other similar blossoms can be substituted—a camellia works fairly well. The real joy comes in making the dolls, not so much in handling them later.

Certainly not edible, though still made from a food, is the figure in Plate 264. Alison Law, a fourth-grader, found that the bubble gum she chewed, then left to dry, still had a bit of flexibility to it. It would never occur to anyone but a child that discarded gum had sculptural potential! It is not a recommended medium, at least from a sanitary point of view, but children's creative urges are rarely stifled by a mere concern for cleanliness.

Macaroni, also a perishable food, can be used for temporary toys. The raw macaroni accepts dye readily and retains a brilliant translucent glow. Mix food coloring and alcohol, since this combination dries faster and sogs less. To dye, mix coloring and macaroni the way you'd

266 (Below) Macaroni, matchboxes, paper straws, and toothpicks are assembled to make colorful wagons. By Ruth Law.

267 (Bottom) Joey, Jimmy, and Janet Tebelskis, ages nine through twelve, assembled this variety of vehicles from macaroni and matchboxes in a matter of minutes.

268–71 Jack-o'-lanterns, carved
from pumpkins, glow from the
lighted candles set inside.

mix butter and popcorn. Then spread on a cookie sheet to dry. The wagons in Plate 266 and Color Plate 43 are made with macaroni wheels, toothpick axles, and empty match boxes. Common household white glue is used to adhere them. Another series made by children is shown in Plate 267.

Among the most appealing of all ephemeral toys are those in which a group can participate. The pooling of energy in the creative production of a snow man makes it an exciting event, even though the figure will soon melt. Sand castles, similarly, will disappear with high tide. The transitory nature of the structure doesn't detract from the total enthusiasm and joy devoted to its building.

Jack-o'-lanterns, also ephemeral, intrigue would-be sculptors of all ages. The idea of permanence is unimportant in the midst of creative excitement—active involvement in the production is what counts. All ephemeral toys have their greatest value in their temporary nature, which focuses attention on doing, not having.

272 Most people never outgrow the fun of building a sand castle, even though it will disappear with high tide.

273, 274 *Children playing on a slide improvised of wood crates and conveyor-belt rollers.*

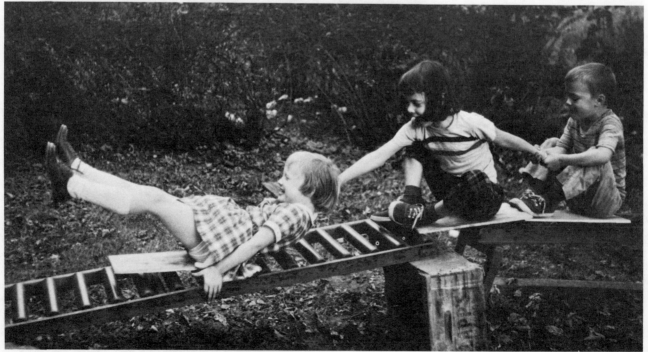

A Gallimaufry . . .

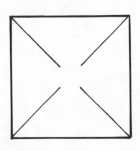

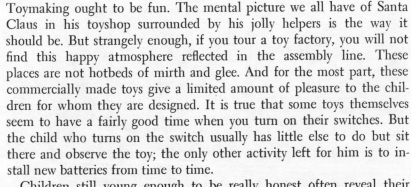

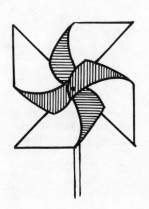

Toymaking ought to be fun. The mental picture we all have of Santa Claus in his toyshop surrounded by his jolly helpers is the way it should be. But strangely enough, if you tour a toy factory, you will not find this happy atmosphere reflected in the assembly line. These places are not hotbeds of mirth and glee. And for the most part, these commercially made toys give a limited amount of pleasure to the children for whom they are designed. It is true that some toys themselves seem to have a fairly good time when you turn on their switches. But the child who turns on the switch usually has little else to do but sit there and observe the toy; the only other activity left for him is to install new batteries from time to time.

Children still young enough to be really honest often reveal their true criteria for toys when they lay aside the superdeluxe, razzle-dazzle mechanical contrivance and play instead with the box it came in. The real challenge in making a toy for a child then is to design one at least as alluring, interesting, and fun as a cardboard carton.

One looks at the children at play on the improvised roller coaster in Plates 273 and 274 and you know that a child-active toy is superior to a toy-active toy. The squeals and laughter of the children on their casually assembled crates and conveyor belt brought the passing photographer to watch and photograph the fun.

A possible exception to the toy-active concept might be Ike Farley at seventy-nine leaning back in his lawn chair to watch his handiwork perform in a good stiff breeze. The unusual wind toys shown in Plates 275 through 277 are Mr. Farley's way of preserving his childhood memories of events in pioneer life at Laton, California, during the first decade of this century. Plate 275 shows his older brother trimming willow logs to be cut by his father and grandfather on the two-man crosscut saw. He assures us that they did indeed smoke their pipes while they worked. Plate 277 shows the mother in her poke bonnet doing the laundry for her family of six—using tub, washboard, and home-made soap. Mr. Farley is shown in Plate 276 with his array of wind-mills. His father was a sawmill hand, a bronco buster, banjo player,

275 Windmill on left turns, causing father to move two-man saw, which activates grandfather, whose motion activates brother with ax chopping wood. Tail blade on far right keeps propeller headed into the wind. By Ike Farley.

276 Ike Farley and his collection of autobiographical wind toys.

277 Turning fan sets the mother's back in motion so that she moves up and down scrubbing clothes.

278 *Stagecoach made entirely of toothpicks by John A. Johnson.*

279 *Display of architectural structures made with toothpicks, also made by John A. Johnson.*

and cattle raiser. Surely such a versatile man must have made a few toys for his four sons; we can't help wondering what they were.

The toys shown in Plates 280 through 283, plus 285, suggest some unusual ideas for fabric toys. The bean-bag rocket (Plate 285) is one of several used in conjunction with a large map of the moon and was made at the time of the first moon landing. Fabric pages with appliqué shapes and objects make an exceptionally durable book. Two pieces of fabric 10″ by 16″ may be sewed together and folded to make four pages of 10″ by 8″, as in Plates 280 and 281. All four pages should have the decorative work applied before the pages are finally sewed together and folded. The work shown here includes machine stitching, hand sewing, embroidery, and fabric appliqué. Plate 283 shows an unsewn page from another appliqué book. Hammers (Plate 289) sewn from printed cotton and stuffed are more suitable for tickling than for pounding.

280 Title page of Alison's Book uses machine zigzag stitching on linen. 8″ by 11″, by Jean Ray Laury.

281, 282 Pages from Alison's Book show appliqué and embroidery work in pictures.

283 Pages of another cloth picture book. Appliqué work is done on fabric before pages are sewn face to face and turned right side out.

284 *Race car whistle (underneath view) showing wood-carver's signature. By Bill Horgos.*

285 *Red, white, and blue rocket is part of a moonshot bean-bag toss game. 6" long, by Mark Law.*

286 *One-eyed bear train whistle. Mouthpiece is at engine cab; tone control in wheels. 4", by Bill Horgos.*

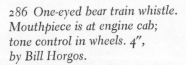

287 *Carved walnut whistle, with ebony and ivory trim. 5", by Bill Horgos.*

151

Some people seem to wear humor-tinted glasses: They "see" funny. It is their outlook on life. No one has to tell Bill Horgos what's funny—he knows it in his bones. His great sense of humor offsets the many cuts on his fingers from whistle-whittling. Plate 287 shows a whistle of ivory, ebony, and walnut. Drawing 47 shows the essentials of a willow or bamboo whistle. A common clay whistle is shown in Drawing 48. Bill Horgos' whistles have the essentials and work well, but they go far beyond that. From woods such as ebony, persimmon, and lignum vitae, he carves elaborate tone-changing holes in his elaborate whistles. The one-eyed bear train whistle in Plate 286 has tone-changing holes in the wheels.

Teakwood and walnut were used to make the handsome rattles in Plate 290. A block of wood was cut apart and hollowed out, then glued back together with a marble inside for a noisemaker. The rattle was then turned on the lathe.

The whirl toys in Plates 288 and 291 make similar use of centrifugal force created by twirling the toy. One is turned on a wood lathe, and the other is made of metal rings assembled on a spindle.

A generous assortment of scrap material went into the making of the witches' gingerbread house shown in Plate 293. The house is made

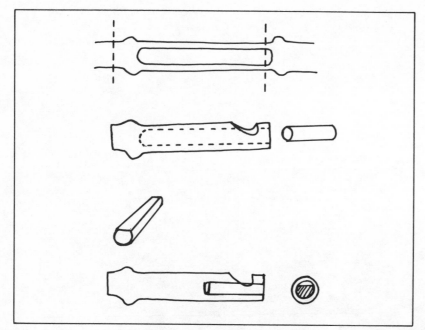

Drawing 47 Use hollow section between joints for bamboo whistle. Whittle a flattened tight plug for mouthpiece. Air hole must be small.

Drawing 48 Whistle may be fashioned as hollow clay figures. Mouthpiece and air hole are essential. The tone-changing hole on top is optional.

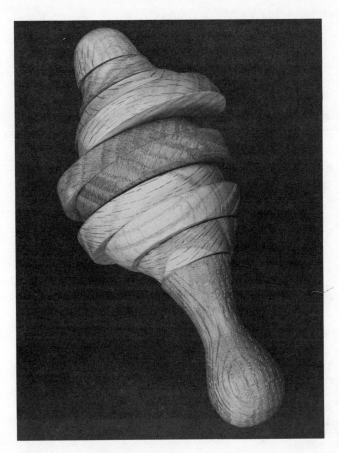

288 Turned hardwood toy uses
slices with large holes drilled in
center, then replaced on spindle.
Hold rattlelike toy in hand and
whirl in a circular motion.
By Gordon Brofft.

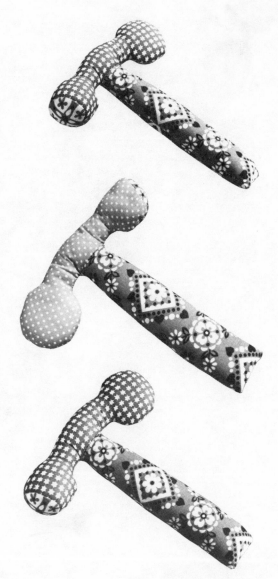

289 Stuffed fabric hammers,
by Lenore Schwartz Goodell.

290 Turned hardwood rattles use
marbles in hollowed out interiors.
By Gordon Brofft.

291 *Patterns of art nouveau shapes change as this toy is whirled in the hand. Rings are sawed from sheet metal by Doug Hansen.*

292 *Log cabin village, made from prunings which Ike Farley found too good to throw away.*

293 *(Opposite) Front door opens on apprentice witch, standing within eating distance of cinnamon hearts and Lifesavers. By Ruth Law.*

154

of large sheets of cardboard reinforced with 2″ by 2″s. Lifesavers and redhots are sawed from Cellotex. Shoebox lids were turned into Hershey bars, and pressed paper plates painted in after-dinner-mint pastels form the roof. All are painted in candy colors and assembled with household glue.

The perfectly detailed little log cabins in Plate 292 are the work of Ike Farley, who felt that the large quantity of tree prunings he had were too good to waste. The logs are meticulously cut and fitted together, then topped off with a slab roof. Each house is equipped with its own stone fireplace chimney.

Log cabins and gingerbread houses are not everyone's idea of a perfect private niche. Some find that having a giant nest in the grass next door to a dragonfly (Plate 294) offers quiet seclusion. One wonders what instinct prompted Elsbeth Ramos' nest—stuffed, lined with velvet, and completed with egg pillows. Some people prefer a cocoon, as evidenced by the work shown in Plate 295. The 6′ high cocoon with an exotic moth hovering in the background suggests a very snug shelter, indeed. Toymakers are quite different from one another, but obviously they bring to their work, first and foremost, a sense of playfulness, of pleasure, and of amusement.

294 (Opposite) A lady laughed and made a real nest for herself using a stuffed coil made of fabric strips, then furnished it with egg pillows. 4′ diameter, by Elsbeth Ramos.

295 Metamorphoses, anyone? Inviting 6′ cocoon of wrapped work with stuffed moth, by Nancy and Dewey Lipe.

157

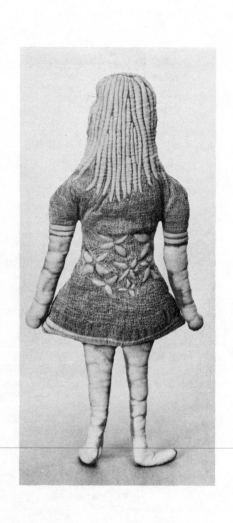

Appendix

CONTRIBUTING TOYMAKERS, ARTISTS AND DESIGNERS

Aidan, Char, Guerneville, Cal.
Aiken, Jim, Clovis, Cal.
Aiken, Joel, Clovis, Cal.
Barnard, Bets, San Diego, Cal.
Barricklow, Jeri, Northridge, Cal.
Bell, Carolyn, Seattle, Wash.
Bitters, Lydia, Fresno, Cal.
Bitters, Stan, Clovis, Cal.
Blair, Margot Carter, San Francisco, Cal.
Bonner, Helen Rene, Fresno, Cal.
Borgeson, Eric, Portland, Ore.
Brofft, Gordon, Brookdale, Cal.
Burke, Bill, New Paltz, N.Y.
Burke, Edd, New Paltz, N.Y.
Cadman, Jane, Claremont, Cal.
Columbini, Rick, Corte Madera, Cal.
Crossland, Jude, Cardiff, Wales, U.K.
Darnley, Sandra, Los Angeles, Cal.
Davis, Lenore, Buffalo, N.Y.
Denny, Rob, Victoria, B.C., Canada
Draughn, Vella, Clovis, Cal.
Dupzyk, Roger, Fresno, Cal.
Farley, Ike, Fresno, Cal.
Floyd, Terrie Sullivan, Malibu, Cal.
Freund, Tom, Vallecitos, N.M.
Fuller, Elizabeth, Claremont, Cal.
Fuller, James, Claremont, Cal.
Goodell, Lenore Schwartz, Placitas, N.M.
Gordon, David, Playa Del Rey, Cal.
Graybill, Richard, Santa Cruz, Cal.

Gurule, Kay, Los Angeles, Cal.
Hansen, Becky, Toledo, Ohio
Hansen, Doug, Fresno, Cal.
Honmyo, Sachi, Palo Alto, Cal.
Horgos, Bill, San Francisco, Cal.
House, Jody, Davis, Cal.
Hughes, Michael, Friendsville, Tenn.
Johansen, Marlo, Fresno, Cal.
Johnson, John A., Sanger, Cal.
Kavanaugh, Babs, Oakland, Cal.
King, David R., Pomona, Cal.
Kwong, Maria, Los Angeles, Cal.
Kwong, Poppy, Los Angeles, Cal.
Lariviere, Marian, Concord, Cal.
Laury, Jean Ray, Clovis, Cal.
Laury, Liz, Clovis, Cal.
Laury, Tom, Clovis, Cal.
Law, Alison, Claremont, Cal.
Law, Hilary Jean, Claremont, Cal.
Law, Mark, Claremont, Cal.
Law, Ruth, Claremont, Cal.
LeCoq, Chris, Seattle, Wash.
Lind, Arthur, Portland, Ore.
Lipe, Nancy and Dewey, Stanford, Cal.
Lundgren, Jorjanna, San Diego, Cal.
Martin, Jude, Oakridge, Tenn.
McLeod, Betsy, Claremont, Cal.
McNutt, Cass, Visalia, Cal.
McNutt, Gloria, Visalia, Cal.
McNutt, Tamelin, Visalia, Cal.
Miller, Margaret, "Mog," Fresno, Cal.
Morrison, Susan, Reno, Nev.
Nassé, Charles, Los Angeles, Cal.

Nassé, Lilo, Los Angeles, Cal.
Northup, Nancy, Woodland, Cal.
Northup, Wendy, Woodland, Cal.
Oltman, Paul and Nancy, Seal Rock, Ore.
O'Mura, H., San Francisco, Cal.
Pahl, Cora, Pomona, Cal.
Parmeter, Doug, Portland, Ore.
Parmeter, Joyce Bossom, Portland, Ore.
Peirano, J. R., Pleasant Hill, Cal.
Peters, Jerri, Fresno, Cal.
Petersen, Ingrid, Claremont, Cal.
Peterson, Alice H., Santa Cruz, Cal.
Pettit, Florence, Glenbrook, Conn.
Ramos, Elsbeth, Rancho Palos Verdes, Cal.
Schneider, Kay, San Luis Obispo, Cal.
Sher, Pipa, Oakland, Cal.
Smalley, Gayle, Fresno, Cal.
Smith, Cam, Los Angeles, Cal.
Smith, Sherman, Midvale, Utah
Spoecker, Janet, Joshua Tree, Cal.
Sutton, Annette, Manhattan Beach, Cal.
Swift, Shippen, Waitsfield, Vt.
Tebelskis, Joey, Jimmy and Janet, Fremont, Cal.
Thorburn, Craig, Clovis, Cal.
Vermeer, Jackie, Sand Point, Ida.
Voight, Jan, Novato, Cal.
Weldon, Joan, LaVerne, Cal.
Wetherby, Sally, Mill Valley, Cal.

MODELS

Atwell, Demian
Bitters, Stan
Delman, Sherman
Denny, Alex
Denny, Angus
Edwards, Mark
Farley, Ike
Fats the Cat
Gibson, Samantha

Johnson, John A.
Kwong, Maria
Laury, Liz
Law, Alison
Law, Hilary Jean
Law, Ruth
Lester, Michael
Morrison, David
Nassé, Sendu Bogi
Nordfors, Erica

Pahl, Becky
Parmeter, Ingrid
Parmeter, Kirstin
Ramos, Sofia
Ray, Alice
Vermeer, David
Vermeer, Kristi
Wiens, Andrew
Wolfe, Daryl

PHOTOGRAPHERS

Beeching, Robert	Color Plate 15
Bitters, Stan	35–37, 42, 177, 227, 233, 252, 268–271, 293, Color Plates 6, 8
Blumenthal, Thomas	10
Burke, Bill	210, Color Plates 34, 39
Burke, Edd	196, 197, Color Plate 46
Carofano, Ray	294, Color Plate 41
Cook, Ted	29, 123, 130, Color Plate 33
Crossland, Jude	Color Plate 25
Darnley, Sandra	69
Denny, Rob	Frontis, 3, 204, 207, 209
Eccles, Dave	1
Floyd, Richard	Color Plates 30, 31
Fresno Bee, The	278, 279
Freund, Tom	Color Plate 36
Goodell, Lenore Schwartz	30, 124, 125, 194
Gross, Richard	156
Hallas, Jim	126, 127
Hughes, Michael	7
Johnson, Beverly Edna	34, 132
Jones III, De Witt	Color Plates 26, 28
Kephart, Richard	225
Kwong, Sam	18
Law, Ruth Milliken	188, 248
Laury, Jean Ray	4, 25, 70, 82, 83, 86, 129, 212, 215, 216, 218, 219, 242, 243, 247, 249–251, 253, 256–258, 264, 265, 272, 289, Color Plates 24, 29, 32
Lind, Arthur	64, 152, 226
Lipe, Dewey	295
McNutt, Gloria	32
Meier, Lee	203
Parmeter, Doug	31, 175, 201, 202, 205, 208
Peirano, J. R.	198
Rush, Beverly	176, 206
Smalley, Gayle	All photographs unless otherwise credited
Smith, Cam	95, 103–105, 128, 159, 190, 200, 261 263, Color Plate 35
Wetherby, Jim	62, 63, 65–68
Wilson, Howard	181

160

DATE DUE

JAN 21 '76			
JAN 28 '77			
JAN 12 '79			
OCT 4 '79			
JAN 3 '80			
OCT 27 '80			
JAN 19 '82			
OCT 20 '82			
OCT 20 '83			
61 JUN			

PRINTED IN U.S.A.